grieving *the* Child
I never knew

Also by Kathe Wunnenberg

Grieving the Loss of a Loved One

Kathe Wunnenberg

grieving *the* Child
I never Knew

A DEVOTIONAL COMPANION FOR COMFORT IN THE
LOSS OF YOUR UNBORN OR NEWLY BORN CHILD

ZONDERVAN™

GRAND RAPIDS, MICHIGAN 49530 USA

ZONDERVAN™

Grieving the Child I Never Knew
Copyright © 2001 by Kathe Wunnenberg

Requests for information should be addressed to:

Zondervan, *Grand Rapids, Michigan 49530*

ISBN 0-310-22777-1

This edition printed on acid-free paper.

Interior design by Todd Sprague

Printed in the United States of America

03 04 05 06 / DC/ 10 9 8 7 6 5

To my children I never knew but who have left an eternal imprint in my life:
Zachary, John Samuel, Luke, and Matthew
And to yours…

Elizabeth Escabedo-Frank

Morgan and Laura Tucker

Linda Watkins

Rachel Maynard

Kristina and Christian Visscher

Cheyenne Cacciatore

Davis Haugen

William and Kelsey Moore

Joshua Sexton

Tina Ramsey

Scott and Jodi Winters

Garrett Mann

Jacob Snider

Noel Saake

Austin Johnson

Genia Campbell

Jonathan Timmer

Baby Young

Baby Miller

Molly Dawn Waltman

Baby Larsen

Baby Johnson

Baby Luczek

Baby Perry

Reed Hamilton

Daniel Weinhold

Baby Sankovich

Baby Hays

Laura and Danny Bullock

Sarah Jennan Holt

Baby Emmorey

Baby Gritter

Baby Hancock

Baby Homan

Baby Baumli

Baby Kent

Baby Bullock

Baby Frank

Baby Berens

Baby Leinart

Pete Ernie Lawson

Austin Johnson

Rebekah Podvaski

Gregory Clay

Baby Mooney

Charles Cheek

Baby Stevens

Baby Wood

Lisa Bullock

Evan King

Holly Beth Mondigran

Gary Tuttle

Katelyn Malm

Baby Gonzales

Baby Verbrugge

Vincent Michael Comacho

Baby Nichols

Baby Carpenter

Baby Fox

Baby Darr

Baby Besher

Ellorie Paige Bos

Daniel Mouser

CONTENTS

• • •

ACKNOWLEDGMENTS

"ARE YOU OVER IT yet?"

Those words still make me cringe. I don't know if I'll ever get over losing my children, though I wish it were that simple. My wounded heart is *healing* but still has a scar.

That's why it took me longer to complete this book than I planned and why it was so painful to write. I *thought* my scar was healed and God could use me to help others grow through the pain of loss. I never expected Him to use my book to help *me* grow too. But He did. Quite frankly, this book came as a "surprise" to me. Like an unexpected pregnancy, I was shocked when my editor called and asked if I would consider writing a second book after my first one, *Grieving the Loss of a Loved One.*

God never ceases to amaze me in how He chooses to work and bring healing into our lives. I didn't expect each story that others shared with me about their loss to rip open the scar in my heart. But each story did. God is the Author of my life, so why should I be surprised that He would choose to use a book to communicate His truth to me.

During one of my writer's blocks I prayed that God would give me creativity to write. Instead, I got a toothache and had to put my writing "on hold" a couple of days until I saw the dentist. I discovered I needed a new filling because of hidden decay. As a result, I wrote "Hidden Unforgiveness." He used my dentist to support me in this book! My dentist trip was a timely reminder that I needed to examine myself for hidden unforgiveness. Ironically, God brought to mind a person whom I needed to forgive. Ouch! My scar ripped open.

Another week I was so busy that I didn't have time to think or feel. *How can I possibly fit writing into my schedule, God?* I prayed. But He gently reminded me that I was hiding and making excuses not to write because it would open the scar in my heart. And He was right. That's why I wrote "Missing in Action" and "It's Pitcher-Filling Time!"

Friends invited our family to spend time away in the mountains so that I could write, but I never opened my laptop once. I felt so guilty about it that when I returned, I wrote "Why Do I Feel So Guilty?" The scar in my heart ripped open again.

I took my son's birthday off from writing to visit his grave. I expected my scar to rip open that day, but it didn't. It happened the next day when my husband and I disagreed about something and I exploded! "Forgiving Others," "Journey to the Snowdrift of Forgiving Yourself," and "Husbands and Wives Grieve Differently" were the outcome.

My mother flew out to lend a domestic hand so I could focus on writing the book. She contracted an upper respiratory infection from my son. That's how "Do You Want to Get Well?" was inspired.

By the time I reached the "final four" devotions to complete, I felt weary. I gave myself a pick-me-up and called my friend Lisa to brainstorm with me, and she gave me just the right insights. "Journey Through the Seasons of Friendship" was born as I realized I was in a season of "shutdown" with most of my friends during this season of writing. Ouch! Thank God for faithful friends.

The writing of the final devotion, "I'll Know My Child in Heaven," was a tender time for me. Somehow it meant putting closure to this book, the baby I had labored so hard to produce. I realized that the process of writing this book was more than just completing a project, it was a necessary part of God's healing process for me in my own grief journey. Ironically, as I mail my final manuscript to my editor, it's just a few days before Mother's Day. Will the scar from my losses ever fully heal? Maybe not in this lifetime, but in heaven it will. For now, God has opened my heart to a new understanding of who He is through the people, stories, places, and circumstances He allowed me to encounter during my writing. He is my Hope, my Healer, and my life's Editor.

I am grateful to those who were with me, supported me, or cheered me on in the journey of writing this book:

   my prayer team — you were my foundation;

my mom, Alice Stephens — not only did you provide meals, but you provided food for my soul and book;

my friend Lisa Jernigan — you are my "intense stabilizer";

Jan James — my friend in the fire who shares August 22;

Jacque DeGideo — my long-distance gutty buddy;

Diane Larson-Lippard and Carol Flowers — your calls and cards kept me going;

C. J. Beals, Greg James, Ginger Smith, Mary Jane Farr, Susan Liming, Diane Markins, Janet Drez, Sherrana O'Donnell, Nancy Tucker, Kendra Hinderland, Darlene Adams, Marlae Gritter, Karen Howells, Sandy Austin, Kim Moore, John and Judy Holly, Laurie Ficarra, Diane Valenti, Joanne Sullins, Carol Poore, Ranee Malina, Patty and Lucy Lira, Barb Tuttle, and Stephanie Snider;

CBWA, my cousin Crystal Stacks, The Vision Group, and Mountain Park Community Church — your prayers and support lifted me;

Dr. Joseph Hanss, my doctor;

Maria La Fond, Joanne Cacciatore, Doreen Sexton, Jennifer Saake, and Fran Rybank — thanks for sharing your resources;

the musicians listed in my resource section . . . when all I could do was listen . . . your songs lifted me to hope again;

my mentors — Carol Kent, Judy Couchman, Carol Travilla, Moms In Touch International, Margie Erbe, Dottie Escabedo-Frank, Jennie Young, the University of Missouri, John McAdam, and Dr. Michael Tucker;

my Zondervan family — my editor Cindy Hays, your caring heart and gentle coaching encouraged me to stretch myself and expose my heart, my editor Verlyn Verbrugge, thanks for your finishing touches, and Ann Spangler and the marketing and sales teams for seeing the need for this book;

my family and friends in Missouri;

Jake and Josh, thanks for sharing Mommy;

and my husband, Rich, who willingly started many days in tears by reading every devotion — you are the wind beneath my wings, who allowed me to slip away writing into the night to soar to new heights.

A special thanks belongs to Mark and Karen Tucker and to Dr. Walter Lippard III for allowing me to share your stories. I appreciate all of the men, women, and children who gave me valuable insights and opened their hearts to me by sharing their personal stories. Your stories touched my life deeply. It's comforting to know that we have "Playmates in Heaven."

And to you, the reader, thank you for opening the pages of this book. When I felt discouraged and wanted to give up, I kept picturing you reading this book, seeking comfort for your soul, and I knew the labor was worth it. Please know that behind every story in my book is another story. And behind the stories is a personal God, who knew just how to lovingly encourage me to press on toward the finish. He will do the same for you. I hope you are pointed to Him through these pages. He gave me the strength to complete this book. He deserves the credit. And Jesus gives us this promise in his Word, that "he who began a good work [of healing] in you will carry it on to completion until the day of Christ Jesus" (Phil. 1:6).

Seven Ways to Use This Book

Grieving the Child I Never Knew is not a how-to book with pat answers about grieving the loss of a child. My hope is that this book will become your personal companion. Think of it as your trusted friend, who walks beside you and gives you permission to be who you are and where you are in your journey. If you are hiding your pain or hiding from people, then discover how God will meet you in your isolation. If you are suffering and need to cry, then weep with all your heart. If you feel like relating to others to help them through a similar journey, then connect. And if you are seeking hope, help, and healing to press on in your future, then start today.

Whether you've recently suffered loss or lost a child long ago, my prayer is that *Grieving the Child I Never Knew* will be a tool to guide you to a deeper understanding of who God is and will meet you in the pain of your loss and point you to Him.

Grieving the Child I Never Knew contains thirty-one devotions divided into six parts. Each devotion contains a Scripture passage, practical/biblical illustration, prayer, discussion questions, and journal section. Part 7 includes a "sharing your personal story" devotional. Additional resources and support organizations are listed at the back of the book to connect you to others who may encourage you in your healing journey.

How you choose to use this book depends on your unique personality, needs, and desired outcomes. Consider the following possible "settings" and choose the one that feels most comfortable to you.

Your 31-Day Companion. Your devotional can be your personal companion for the next month. Whether you choose to curl up with your book in bed each night, start your day with it at the breakfast table, or take a break with it at work, it's up to you. You decide the time and place.

Quick Pick-Me-Up. Sitting on the coffee table is your devotional companion, ready and available for you to pick up when questions or emotions surface and you need a quick dose of encouragement. Use the Table of Contents as a compass to guide you to the reading that meets your needs in the moment.

Table for Two. Heartfelt conversation with another person can double your insights, laughter, and tears. Sitting with someone can give you courage and motivation to finish the book. Who will join you at the table? Your spouse? Friend? Neighbor? Coworker? Family member? Pastor? Counselor? The person you know who lost a child?

Grief Group Guide. Your devotional can be a tool to facilitate grief discussions in small or large groups. The options are endless in using this material. Choose the format, readings, and number of weeks that meet your group's need. Interactive learning can be encouraging and open your eyes to a variety of perspectives

Small Group Bible Study. Use the devotional as a six-week Bible study for anyone who desires to know more about grieving the loss of a child. Focus on one section per week. Have your group memorize Scripture(s) from the readings.

A Gift That Lasts. Someone you know has lost a child. Make this devotional companion your standard gift for the bereaved. Share how this book has encouraged you in your journey.

A Resource Book for Pastors/Counselors. When someone dies, pastors and counselors are usually the first people called. This devotional guide can accompany them as they meet with the bereaved and can be given as a gift that says they care.

READINGS FOR SPECIAL DAYS OR NEEDS

SPECIAL OCCASIONS, HOLIDAYS, AND personal circumstances may trigger your grief and expose a new dimension of grieving your child. When you encounter these times in your journey and desire encouragement or a fresh perspective, turn to the selected reading for that specific day or need.

INTRODUCTION

   • • •

I NEVER KNEW THIS child fully, so why do I grieve so deeply? I never held this tiny baby, never saw the sleeping face, never locked eyes and gazed into the soul of this little person. Yet, I feel as if a part of me died and left a void in my being. Most people don't seem to understand and minimize my loss instead of validating my pain from losing this nameless child. Will I always feel so lonely and misunderstood? Is it normal to mourn someone I never knew or lost so long ago? How can I move beyond the hurt and begin to hope again? Only when I gave myself permission to grieve the loss of my child did I begin to pick up the pieces of my broken heart and start to heal.

My journey through grieving the child I never knew began when I stepped back through my memories to a time early in my marriage when my husband and I decided to start a family. I expected to have a child within a year, just like everyone else I knew. To my surprise, I discovered that conceiving a child didn't come easily for me. Two years, numerous doctor's visits, months of temperature charts, and many ovulation kits later, I discovered I was finally pregnant just days before Christmas in 1987. I didn't realize at the time that God would use this unknown child to penetrate my heart and draw me close to Him in a way I had never experienced.

When I lost our baby on my husband's thirtieth birthday, I was disappointed but didn't feel deeply about this loss. Why should I? I never knew this child. Unaware that my pain was hidden and my journey through grief had already begun, I pressed on in life.

In 1989 God fulfilled the desires of our heart and His plan by providing us Jake through a Christian adoption agency. When Jake began to pray for "a baby to grow in Mommy's belly," I was shocked. But he persisted. A couple of years later when I went to the doctor for the "flu," he announced, "You're pregnant!" Jake knew that God had answered his prayer.

But on Good Friday of 1996, our family stared at the monitor in disbelief, realizing our unborn baby had a fatal birth defect. I found myself in my own Garden of Gethsemane, crying out, "God, please take this cup of suffering from me!" By Easter morning I released my anguish and my unborn child into His care. "Not my will, but thine be done!"

During the long months of waiting on the birth of my baby, God worked through this child to teach me many life lessons. On different days I laughed, cried, learned the necessity of silence and solitude, released control, allowed others to encourage me, and saw my faith soar. I tasted humility and surrender, and I learned what it means to enjoy every moment. I learned how precious praying friends are, and I learned how faithful and loving God is to care about me personally.

I didn't know what the future held, but I was certain of *who* held the future. I believed God was able to heal my child — and I proclaimed that publicly. Yet I also knew that if He chose not to, I would praise Him anyway! On August 22, 1996, our son John Samuel was born with eyes looking up at God. His birth was a celebration of God's love and a testimony of the value of every life. Within a few hours heaven's gates opened and welcomed him into the arms of Jesus. His brief life touched thousands of people with the reality of God, and the ripple effects will only be known in eternity.

A few months later I discovered I was pregnant again. *How caring of God to bless me with another child!* I thought. But I never got to know this child or hold this baby in my arms. A few weeks into my pregnancy, I miscarried. My heart was breaking for all three children I had lost.

Then a few months later, I discovered I was pregnant again! *Surely God will allow me to keep this child!* I thought. But He didn't. On Christmas Eve of 1997, I lost this child too. *Where are You, God?* I cried out. God used this fourth child I lost to help me grieve openly and share my pain with others through writing about grief.

In July of 1998, I confirmed that I was pregnant with a fifth child. I was terrified at the thought of another loss. But God overshadowed my fear with faith to trust Him yet another time. In March of 1999 Joshua Paul was born — after nearly nineteen years of marriage. I never expected to be forty and writing a book, with a baby in my arms. But I am. What a journey!

Although my journey is different from yours and I may never fully understand everything you are feeling, I can relate to some of your pain. Behind the pages of this book is an ordinary woman, a fellow griever, still in the journey of grieving the loss of four children. And behind the woman is a faithful God who has made this book possible. My prayer is that *Grieving the Child I Never Knew* will help point you to God and that you will experience His presence in the midst of your pain. Let's begin the healing journey...

"Yes, you're pregnant!"

Do you remember hearing those words or seeing the positive results from a test? What was your reaction? Your response to the news of expecting a child is a lot like riding a roller coaster.

Some people respond with enthusiasm. They've longed to experience this ride and have anxiously awaited their turn. "Let's celebrate! We're finally on!" they shout. They race to the front of the roller coaster, ready to embrace the thrill of their lifetime.

Others hear the news and board the ride a bit cautious and reluctant. Seated a few rows from the front, they look nervous. They've been on the ride before but never made it to the end. Strapped in by fear and uncertainty, they cling to the hope that they'll complete the ride this time.

A third group of riders sit in the middle section of the coaster. They sport that "in-between look" — neither happy nor sad — as if they could take this ride or leave it. Some suspect these folks are in shock and don't believe it's true, perhaps because they've waited such a long time to get on and never thought they would get on the coaster.

At the back of the coaster sit another cluster of people. Like the first three groups, they are executives, homemakers, students, unemployed, married, single, young, old, rich, and poor. Jolted by the unexpected news or the loop-to-loop of their circumstances, they look as if they are about to get sick. Their solemn faces are powdered with disappointment, dread, and disbelief. "I can't believe I let this happen!" "I don't want a child!"

Maybe you can picture yourself with one of the groups. Although each of our circumstances, stories, and responses are different, most of you who hold this book share a common bond: never getting to the end of the ride, the loss of never fully knowing your child. Maybe you just started your journey clicking down the track and your coaster derailed when you were told, *"Your HCG levels are decreasing and you will miscarry,"* or *"Your baby is growing outside your womb and emergency surgery is the only hope to save your life."* Or were you well on your way to the end of the ride when your doctor told you the ride is over because *"I cannot detect a heartbeat"*? Did you perhaps make it to the end of the ride but shortly after getting off your baby died? Or maybe you didn't want to be on the ride in the first place. A baby was not in your plans, and now your guilt for feeling that way is making you sick.

You have lost a child. So have I. Regardless of the circumstances, it's time to begin the process of mending our broken hearts. Join me in the journey through grief as we face our loss together and look to God to guide us through.

HIDING

Hiding: *to put out of sight; to conceal for shelter or protection; to keep secret*

Rock of Ages, cleft for me,
Let me hide myself in Thee.

A. M. TOPLADY

For you created my inmost being;
  you knit me together in my mother's womb.
I praise you because I am fearfully and wonderfully made;
  your works are wonderful,
  I know that full well.
My frame was not hidden from you
  when I was made in the secret place.
When I was woven together in the depths of the earth,
  your eyes saw my unformed body.
All the days ordained for me
  were written in your book
  before one of them came to be.

PSALM 139:13–16

Devotion 1

HIDE-AND-SEEK

• • •

Then the man and his wife heard the sound of the LORD God as he was walking in the garden in the cool of the day, and they hid from the LORD God among the trees of the garden. But the LORD God called to the man, "Where are you?"

GENESIS 3:8–9

HIDE-AND-SEEK IS ONE OF my favorite childhood games. I enjoy hiding. Whether I stash myself in a trash can, hang behind the curtains, or pile laundry on top of myself, my goal is to camouflage myself so well that I can't be found. It's always a challenge to remain silent and still when the seek-and-find mission is under way. When footsteps tread close by and the person yells, "Where are you?" I have to make a choice: Will I remain hiding or will I expose myself and be found?

That's the situation that Adam and Eve found themselves in after they disobeyed God and were hiding in the garden. I can only imagine the anguish they must have felt when they realized that "death" was part of their life now. They would experience death *physically* through the aging process, *emotionally* through guilt and shame, *socially* by blaming each other, and *spiritually* by alienating themselves from God because of sin. Picture this bereaved couple, mourning the life they once had and peering out from the bushes, afraid they would be discovered and forced to face the truth.

Like Adam and Eve, you, too, have experienced a great loss. Whether through miscarriage, stillbirth, tubal pregnancy, or infant death, your loss may cause you to hide physically, emotionally, socially, or spiritually. Sometimes the pain is so intense you may want to discon-nect from others and from God. You look for ways to hide your hurt. You camouflage your questions, fears, and disappointment so well that you may think others do not notice. But how long can you stash your silent heartache? Is hiding really healthy or does it hold you back from a healing journey? Sooner or later someone will come to find you.

Do you find yourself hiding in the bushes like Adam and Eve? The Lord is walking through your garden, calling your name. How will you respond? Will you remain in hiding or will you expose your real feelings about your loss and begin the journey through your grief?

God, the loss of my child is so agonizing. I feel as if I'm playing hide-and-seek with my pain. I've camouflaged my questions, fears, and hurts so that others will not notice and pass me by. How long can I hide my heartache? Will You be my truth today? Reveal the specific areas of my life (physically, emotionally, socially, and spiritually) where I need healing. Show me how to move forward in my grief journey. Amen.

Steps Toward Healing

1. How have you been hiding the pain of your loss?
2. How have you felt disconnected? Physically? Emotionally? Socially? Spiritually?
3. Imagine someone calling out, "Where are you in your grief?" How would you respond today? How would you like to respond a year from now?
4. Are you ready now to take a few steps forward in grieving your child?

My Personal Journey

Devotion 2

JOURNEY TO THE HIDING PLACE

• • •

You are my hiding place;
you will protect me from trouble
and surround me with songs of deliverance.

PSALM 32:7

SIRENS BLARE. THE SKY darkens. Trees rock frantically back and forth. The wind whirls violently. A funnel-shaped cloud descends. All warning signs that a tornado is coming — and you'd better head for cover.

A tornado is a common occurrence in some parts of the United States. Its destructive wind has been known to demolish anything in its path: entire towns, livestock, and countless lives.

While growing up in Missouri, I learned that one of the safest places to be when a tornado hits is in the basement. This below-ground-level storeroom is a place where I weathered many storms and a few tornadoes. Whenever I scurried down the stairs to my hiding place, I felt safe. I had everything I needed: food, water, bedding, flashlights, a radio, a television, and games. Sometimes I even forgot about the storm because I couldn't see it or hear it.

Hidden below the ground, unable to see or hear the storm, I could feel disconnected for minutes or hours. Only after the storm had passed and I ascended the stairs did I have to face the truth. On more than one occasion, what a shock to face reality! Broken tree limbs and debris blanketed our lawn. A pathway through town of uprooted trees and damaged power lines was a vivid reminder of the twister.

At times in your grief journey you may detect a storm is coming. You may sense sirens blaring in your soul. Your mood darkens or you feel frantic. Emotions whirl violently as the reality of your loss starts to descend on you. It's time to head for cover. *To the basement!* you exclaim. You find yourself below the surface of reality, hiding from it. Your "basement" may be activity or exercise or work. Maybe you hide in eating or curling up with a book. Your basement may look different from mine, but each of us has one. A place to hide. You don't have to face the questions, doubts, fears, and guilt. No people to respond to or excuses to make. Disconnected from reality, you may even forget about the storm of your loss.

But the pain of your loss hasn't gone away. With time you must realize you cannot live in the basement forever. When you finally ascend to face reality, you may be surprised to discover shattered dreams, a broken heart, emotional debris, uprooted expectations, and damaged relationships. But you will also find peace in knowing that the storm has passed.

Sure, you may have a lot of cleanup work to do, but there's unlimited eternal aid available. God will help you face the truth and will work with you to repair the storm damage. You will feel safe in His presence and in His Word. He wants to be the One to whom you run for shelter as you continue your journey. Will you let Him be your hiding place?

Lord, help! I'm hiding from the storm of my loss. I admit I've disconnected from reality by hiding my pain in _____. I need Your help to face the truth and to repair the damage that's been done in my life and in the lives of others. Come to my aid. Repair and restore my life. Remind me to run to Your presence and Your Word in my journey through grief. Be my hiding place and help me journey on. Amen.

Steps Toward Healing

1. How do you hide from the storm of your loss?
2. Identify the emotional debris, uprooted expectations, or damaged relationships from your loss in need of being repaired. Write this in a prayer request to God.
3. Picture God as your hiding place. Read Psalm 32:8 aloud as if God were responding to you today.

MY PERSONAL JOURNEY

_____

_____

_____

_____

_____

_____

_____

_____

_____

_____

_____

_____

Devotion 3

FACING THE TRUTH

● ● ●

*Dear friends, do not be surprised at the painful
trial you are suffering, as though something
strange were happening to you.*

1 PETER 4:12

*Send forth your light and your truth,
      let them guide me;
let them bring me to your holy mountain,
      to the place where you dwell.*

PSALM 43:3

HAVE YOU EVER IGNORED the truth about your loss because reality was too painful to face? I have. For a season after my baby's death, coping with people and situations involving babies was challenging for me. I avoided certain activities, friends, restaurants, family, and even church on baby dedication day because I was afraid of how I would react. Making excuses worked for a while, but I realized I couldn't run from every situation and would have to find a way to survive.

One occasion happened a few months after our baby's death, when we took our traditional trip to spend Thanksgiving with family. Ironically, on the previous year's trip I had conceived our child. Not only would I have to confront memories and questioning stares, but also newborn babies and those sporting maternity attire. During this trip, I had several "grief encounter moments" when I hid in the bathroom or mentally escaped.

Was this abnormal behavior? Some may think so. But looking back I realize that my seemingly irrational ways of coping were necessary for me at the time and enabled me to survive and to scale my mountain of grief. Once again the story of a king and two mothers that I shared in my first book, *Grieving the Loss of a Loved One*, comes to mind.

Two women enter a courtroom and stand in front of King Solomon. One holds a baby; the other clings to an empty blanket. The woman with empty arms rushes forward and tells Solomon about her son's birth. She chokes back tears as she shares how the other woman gave birth to a son a few days later. But her baby died. This woman swapped the dead baby for the living baby while the new mother slept. "That's *my* baby," she moans.

Silence pervades the room. The king sees the pain in her eyes. He turns to face the woman holding the baby. She glares at him and shouts, "No, the living one is *my* son and the dead one is *hers*!"

What fear must have come into the heart of the real mother. What boldness and denial were yet in the heart of the mother whose child was dead.

Solomon commands an attendant to bring him a sword. "Divide the living child in two, and give half to the one, and half to the other."

"Oh, my lord, give her the living child and don't kill it," cries the woman with empty arms.

"Divide it!" says the other.

The truth can't be denied. The king, who is the wisest of judges, knows by the two mothers' words who is the real mother.

I can imagine how grateful that woman was as she reached for her baby and held him once again in her arms. Her tears turned to smiles and the heaviness in her heart was replaced with joy.

But what about the other woman? Was she really cruel-hearted and vindictive, or was she a desperate, grieving mother who would do anything to have her baby back?

I can only imagine the shock and pain this mother must have felt when she discovered in the morning that her baby was dead. Did she convince herself he was only sleeping and would wake up soon? How tormenting for her to hear the other baby's healthy cry. No one understood the anguish she felt. She couldn't face her loss. I wonder if she thought that just being near what she longed for would lessen her pain.

Clutching her lifeless baby, she tiptoed into the room where everyone was sleeping. She bent down and peeked at the tiny breathing bundle. This felt so familiar. *I'll pick him up and hold him just for a few minutes,* she thought. She gently laid her baby down and scooped up the living baby into her arms. She didn't remember how long she held him or what happened next. All she knew was joy returned to her heart and a sense of relief that the death was just a terrible nightmare.

I'm not justifying or condoning her actions. Yet I can relate to her pain and understand how grief can drive us to do, think, or say strange things. My brother and his wife had a healthy baby boy just a few days before my son was born and died. Although I was excited for them, the first few times I saw my nephew, he reminded me of what I longed for but didn't have. Sometimes when I held him, I would imagine that this was my son and allowed myself to feel the joy of a new mother, even if only for a few moments.

Now, when I look at my nephew, I see my nephew, a bright, handsome boy who is a sweet reminder to me of the age my son would be. God used him in my journey through denial to fill my empty arms, comfort my grieving soul, and help me to face the reality of my loss.

Fantasizing that your baby is still alive is one way to cope. Sometimes facing reality is too painful and denying your loss is a temporary way to survive. In the right time, God will help you face reality and cope with your loss.

God, it feels like a dream that my child is gone and won't cry to tell me this is only a nightmare. My pain is too raw to face that reality right now. I want to pretend this never happened. It's like I'm standing in a courtroom with the truth on one side of me and denial on the other. You are the wise, discerning judge, and You see my pain and the truth. Help me to cope with the truth. Reveal it to me today. Amen.

Steps Toward Healing

Read the story in 1 Kings 3:16–28.

1. Describe how each woman in the story responded to loss.
2. What would you say to each woman in the story?
3. How have you responded to others who have what you lost?
4. What would you like others to do or say to you?

Don't hide your pain. Be truthful with yourself, God, and others this week.

Seek the listening ear of a person who is compassionate and trustworthy or has experienced loss similar to yours.

MY PERSONAL JOURNEY

FROM MINIMIZING TO VALIDATING

● ● ●

O LORD, you have searched me
and you know me. . . .
My frame was not hidden from you
when I was made in the secret place.

PSALM 139:1, 15

"DON'T CRY OVER A miscarriage. It's God's way of getting rid of something imperfect."

"You can always have another one."

"Be thankful you have other children."

"You have so much going on, now isn't a good time for a baby anyway!"

"Well, maybe it's for the best."

Has anyone made a comment like this to you? If not, sooner or later they might. These words were intended to comfort my husband and me after I miscarried our third baby a few weeks into my pregnancy in 1997. Instead, they intensified our pain by minimizing our loss. I'll never forget the devastating look in my husband's eyes when someone said, "Better to lose *it* now than later!" I was fuming inside and wanted to scream, *My baby was not an "IT"! My baby was a person in the making, an individual just like you!*

Many people feel the trauma and tragedy of the death of adults and young lives — family, friends, neighbors, coworkers, and the community. Obituaries validate their existence. But with a pregnancy loss there are few memories, and the ones that exist live only to the woman and perhaps her husband. Who is this baby anyway? What is his identity? What contributions did she make to society? Many do not acknowledge a developing child as a viable life, and those who do may not understand why this type of individual is so significant and should be mourned.

How are we to grieve about someone whom society does not expect us to grieve? Parents may mourn deeply, little, or not at all. There is no set mold or "right" way for mourning a loss. It is as normal for parents not to grieve as it is for them to be devastated. Those who mourn little or not at all initially may be minimizing their pain and end up mourning the baby months or years later.

That's what happened to me after I miscarried our first child in 1988. Rich and I were having dinner with friends to celebrate his thirtieth birthday. We were excited that I was finally pregnant after years of trying. I excused myself to go to the bathroom. Moments later I knew I was losing our first child.

I resolved that I would not let this circumstance ruin Rich's celebration, so I resumed the party in progress as if nothing had happened. I quickly divorced myself from the disappointment of the miscarriage. I had a strong faith and assured the few friends who knew we had lost the baby that it was God's will and I was fine. I refused to mourn my loss. Instead I minimized it and swept the sorrow of my loss under the rug of my smiles, activity, and work. Although I mouthed the words "I lost a child," the meaning didn't sink in until years later after I suffered the death of our son and my third miscarriage.

Others who have not experienced losing a child will probably not understand how you feel or know how to respond to you. But your mourning does make sense. You lost a child. You have good reason to hurt. Don't minimize your pain! Pour out your heart to God. He understands. He is waiting with open arms to comfort you and validate the sorrow you've been hiding. He created your precious little one and knows your child by name. Let God embrace you with His love and compassion, just as He does your child in His heavenly kingdom.

Lord, should I really be feeling this way about losing my child? Am I making too much out of this loss? I know others don't understand how I feel. Help me to forgive the people who try to minimize my pain. My loss was a child, not a mistake or clump of cells. My child was a part of me. You understand. You created my precious baby. It's comforting to know You saw my child in my womb and know my child by name. My child has value in Your eyes. Give me courage to grieve and validate my pain. You are my Creator, the One who can form my loss into something good in time. Amen.

Steps Toward Healing

1. How have others minimized your loss? How does that make you feel? Why do you feel others responded that way?
2. Read Psalm 139 aloud. What verses validate your child's worth?
3. Often people make hurtful comments because they are uninformed. They may not fully understand that loss is loss and you cannot compare how long you were pregnant or had a child to the grief you may feel. What could others say that would validate your loss?

MY PERSONAL JOURNEY

Devotion 5

MISSING IN ACTION

● ● ●

Be still and know that I am God.

PSALM 46:10

HAVE YOU EVER BEEN so busy that you were unable to think or feel? I have.

Activity distracts me from facing the pain of my loss. In a sense my "to do" list keeps me *missing in action.* The more I do, the less I feel. The less I feel, the less I hurt. Hiding in my foxhole of busyness, I am sheltered from the battle zone of loss. I can avoid the cross fire of people's questions and the emotional explosions from my hurt. Armed with my Daytimer and camouflaged by fatigue, I feel safe.

Unfortunately, I don't realize that I am at war with myself. Rest is my enemy. I convince myself that "busy is better," and the war inside me rages on. Then I'm hit with a missile of reality. It slows me down. I cringe in pain from the flashbacks of my losses.

Since most of my wounds aren't visible from my loss, I ignore them and keep moving. Then another missile of reality hits. My wound of fear is exposed. I'm afraid to face my loss. *Will I lose another child?* Control is my other unhealed battle scar. *I couldn't control my body or the circumstances that led to the loss of my child but I can control my schedule and how I grieve.*

I need to heal, but I don't know how. Will I stay missing in action and delay the healing of my heart and soul, or will I come out of hiding and slow down to face the truth?

During a fourteen-month time frame I lost an infant and had two miscarriages. I didn't realize that I was *missing in action* during that time in my life until I looked back at my Daytimer. My schedule was full. In addition to my job and my role as wife and mother, I juggled more than twenty other roles. Whew! No wonder I was exhausted and didn't have time to think or feel.

Rest was nearly nonexistent. How could I expect myself to heal? At that time I didn't even know that I needed to. I thought I was doing fine and handling my grief in a positive manner. I didn't even realize I needed to slow down until I attended a weekend retreat in the mountains.

Cool air and pine trees replaced my phone and e-mail. One of the planned activities during the weekend was to spend time alone with God. I plopped down beneath a tree by a rushing stream. Then a missile of reality hit my soul. *Be still and know that I am God.*

I began to weep. Then another missile hit this time, exposing the wounds of my loss. *Cast all your cares on Me, because I care for you.*

For the first time in a long time, I had uninterrupted time with God. I poured out my heart to Him about the pain of my loss and my need for Him to help me slow down. That was a defining moment in my journey through grief. I finally acknowledged and faced the pain of the loss I'd been hiding in my activity. I was ready to journey on.

Are you missing in action and unable to heal the wounds from your loss? Have you allowed your activity to replace your sensitivity to your pain? Are you at war with yourself? Maybe it's time to slow down and escape from your Daytimer.

That's what Jesus did after He suffered the loss of His cousin John the Baptist. He released His activity and went away to a lonely place to spend time with God. Learn from His example. Stop hiding in activity. Be still in God's presence. It's a necessary stop in your grief journey.

Lord, please slow me down! I'm missing in action. My schedule is so busy I don't have time to think or feel. Am I hiding in the foxhole from the battle zone of my loss? Let a missile of reality through Your word hit my

soul. Expose the wounds from my loss and heal them. You are the Victor.
Bring peace to the war within my soul so I can journey on. Amen.

Steps Toward Healing

1. Are you too busy? Make a list of your roles and the activities associated with each role in a typical week. Is time alone with God on your list?

2. Do you feel as if you've been avoiding facing your hurt? Why or why not? Why do you think it is so difficult for you to be still?

3. Where is your "foxhole of faith," the physical place you go to "be still" with God? If you don't have a place, where could you go? Read Psalm 46, Matthew 11:28, and Psalm 5.

4. Schedule at least ten minutes each day to be still with God. Take your list of activities to Him and ask Him to show you the roles you need to release for a time.

5. Are there others who can help you face reality and share your load? Who are they?

MY PERSONAL JOURNEY

SUFFERING

Suffering: to endure hardship or suffer loss

Children's Footprints

Some children come into our lives and go quickly.
Some children come into our lives and stay awhile.
All our children come into our lives and leave footprints —
Some oh so small;
Some a little larger;
Some, larger still,
But all have left their footprints on our lives; in our hearts,
And we will never, never be the same.

DOREEN SEXTON

I bear my willing witness that I owe more to the fire, and the hammer, and the file, than to anything else in my Lord's workshop. I sometimes question whether I have ever learned anything except through the rod. When my schoolroom is darkened, I see most.

CHARLES H. SPURGEON

We also rejoice in our sufferings, because we know that suffering produces perseverance; perseverance, character; and character, hope. And hope does not disappoint us, because God has poured out his love into our hearts by the Holy Spirit, whom he has given us.

ROMANS 5:3—5

Devotion 6

NOTHING TO SHOW FOR MY LOSS

• • •

Where does understanding dwell?...
God understands the way to it
and he alone knows where it dwells.

JOB 28:20, 23

WHEN YOU LOSE A child, you feel a poignant pain. Your dream of experiencing your child develop, be born, or grow up is cruelly snatched away. And you may feel as if you have nothing to show for your loss but a stack of bills, an out-of-shape body, raging hormones, an incomplete nursery, pain and suffering, and empty arms. It doesn't seem fair. But we live in a fallen world, and the pain and suffering of that world touches our lives too. Nothing will be totally fair and perfect until we get to heaven.

Since our world is fallen, we are all victims of heartache at one time or another. Your miscarriage, stillbirth, tubal pregnancy, or infant loss isn't a sign of sin in your life or a message from God to "clean up your act." It is simply a form of suffering common to the human experience of living in this world.

When we discovered in the fourth month of my pregnancy that our baby had a fatal defect and would die unless God performed a miracle, I plummeted to a new depth of suffering. I believed God could heal our son and proclaimed this publicly to others. I also predetermined that if He chose not to heal our son, I would praise God anyway.

During the months that followed I endured the skeptical looks of those who thought I was in denial and the pain of being ignored by others. Most days were bittersweet. I cherished every moment my son kicked or the hours he kept me up at night. I talked to him, read to him, and prayed aloud to him. I knew that as long as he was in my womb, he was safe and alive.

When I entered the hospital to be induced at forty-two weeks, I hoped God would answer our prayer and I would bring our healthy, whole baby home. During the long, intensive labor, I suffered the pain of uncertainty, not knowing if my child would live or die. It wasn't until my son was born and the doctor placed him in my arms that I knew that I would have to say "hello" and then "good-bye."

The reality of this suffering didn't impact me until I was alone and looked down at my stomach. I realized my son was gone — and I had nothing to show for my labor or his life except an expanded waistline and a limp blanket. The next day when my husband wheeled me out of the hospital, I felt awkward and empty. My heart ached with certainty knowing my son was with Jesus, but my arms were empty.

Jesus understands your journey through suffering. In the Garden of Gethsemane, He pleaded with God to take His cup of suffering from Him. But He willingly offered to accept His suffering, if that was part of God's plan. He suffered rejection from His friends, physical and emotional abuse, public humiliation, cruel comments, physical torture, and death on a cross. Did He deserve it? No. He was innocent. Yet He knew our world was fallen and there was no hope to redeem humanity's spiritual suffering but for Jesus to die on the cross for our sins.

What if you were to ask Jesus' mother, Mary, "What do you have to show for the loss of your son?" She might reply, "Empty arms and the assurance of living eternally with my son Jesus in heaven." That's the good news about suffering. Jesus has "been there, done that." He can relate to what you're experiencing, but He wants to give you hope to see your loss in the scope of eternity. He is willing to take your cup of suffering and walk with you through your pain. Go ahead, give Him your cup of suffering now. Allow Him to fill your arms with His hope and salvation.

God, my arms are empty. I have nothing to show for my loss and it seems so unfair. I didn't expect things to turn out this way. You could have saved my child, but You didn't. You are the One who understands and sees the big picture, even if I don't. Please take my cup of suffering and walk with me through my pain. Wrap Your arms of understanding and comfort around me. Fill my empty arms with Your hope and salvation. Amen.

Steps Toward Healing

1. Recall the first time after you lost your child when you realized you had "empty arms." What emotions did you encounter?
2. Some women who lost children said that "aching arms" was a common occurrence for them and holding something helped ease the pain. What could you hold?
3. Jesus was innocent, yet willingly suffered and died. How does His example give you hope?

MY PERSONAL JOURNEY

_____

_____

_____

_____

_____

Devotion 7

JOURNEY THROUGH THE DARKNESS
OF DEPRESSION

● ● ●

But you, O LORD, be not far off;
O my Strength, come quickly to help me.

PSALM 22:19

TRACY SAT IN HER office unable to concentrate. She couldn't complete her work regardless of how hard she tried. Over the past several months since losing her baby, careless mistakes and a negative and critical attitude were the norm for her. Exhaustion and a loss of appetite were her constant companions. Her generally positive outlook about people and life in general had faded.

One morning, Tracy couldn't get out of bed. She felt as if all the electricity in her life had been shut off and darkness was closing in. Fear gripped her. She felt so out of control and lost. What was happening to her? She had a strong faith, supportive family, and friends. Known for her optimism and reliance on God, Tracy was the model of physical and spiritual health. But at this moment, Tracy felt weak and alone. She knew something was terribly wrong, but she didn't know how to overcome this personal power outage in her life. She was afraid of what others would think if she cried out for help.

The darkness of depression is common in the journey through grief. Like Tracy, you may be trekking along your lighted path of life and appear unaffected from your loss. You've acknowledged your loss, allowed yourself to grieve, talked about it, gone to support groups, and read Scripture. Maybe you haven't noticed that your attitude, appetite, or ability to cope with everyday activities has dimmed and is getting darker.

Even if you are aware of the changes in your life, you may choose to make excuses or rationalize it away rather than face the darkness of depression that may be closing in. *Good Christians shouldn't struggle with depression,* you think. *Maybe I'm just working too hard or need to exercise more than I am. I know my baby is with God, so I should feel relieved and glad.*

The darkness of depression can occur at any time during your grief journey. It may hit suddenly and severely, like "lights out" in a power outage in a storm, or it may be more gradual, like a dimmer on your light switch. Or you may be one of the fortunate ones who never or only moderately encounter depression.

I used to cringe if someone would ask me, "Kathe, are you depressed?" I felt as if depression meant I was weak or incompetent in some way. "It's probably my hormones," I rationalized. "I'm writing this book, which is really painful." It wasn't until a well-known Christian leader who had also lost a child told me of her depression that I accepted that my angry outbursts, cluttered home, inability to finish projects, forgetfulness, frequent tears, and negative attitude could all be symptoms of depression.

In the dark night of my soul I discovered I was not alone. David penned many of his psalms when he was depressed. Eve must have suffered when one of her sons killed the other. Hannah wept because she desired a child. Elizabeth must have been depressed every month when she discovered she was not pregnant.

Facing the darkness and seeking medical or professional expertise to help you journey through depression is often necessary. God wants to be the light to guide us through. Often in our blackest moments, we discover that His light shines brightest. Ask Him to guide you to others who can help illuminate your path so you can journey on.

God, darkness is closing in on my life. I can't cope with life the way I used to. I need Your help! Help me face my pain. Restore me. Be my light and guide me through the dark night of my soul. Guide me to others who can illuminate my path and help me journey through. Amen.

Steps Toward Healing

1. In what specific ways are you having difficulty coping with life?
2. What steps can you take to seek help?
3. Whom do you know who could brighten your path and help you journey through the dark night of your soul?

MY PERSONAL JOURNEY

Devotion 8

THE EMPTY FRAME

• • •

If we had forgotten the name of our God
or spread out our hands to a foreign god,
would not God have discovered it,
since he knows the secrets of the heart?

PSALM 44:20–21

PAM DISCOVERED SHE WAS pregnant, but before she could share her news with her boyfriend, she lost the baby. *No one needs to know what happened!* she rationalized to herself. Locked in a hidden safe behind the picture of her life was her secret. She didn't want to disappoint her parents, so she vowed never to tell them.

Life continued for Pam. She graduated from college, started a career, married, and had two children. She forgot about the child she'd lost — or so she thought. Until one Thanksgiving.

Pam looked forward to large family gatherings at her mom's. "Going home" for Thanksgiving was the one tradition that *everyone* in her family kept. She could hardly wait to see how much her nieces and nephews had grown since last year.

"We're here!" Pam's children announced as they scurried up the front steps and gave their grandmother a hug. Pam walked inside. The aroma of fresh baked bread and apple pie filled the air. *Mom still remembers my favorites.* Memories flooded her mind of growing up here. She strolled into the living room and spied the old piano. *I wonder if I still remember how to play,* she thought as she sat down and placed her fingers on the ivory keys. To her amazement, she did. She struck the final chord and looked up with a confident glow. An audience of framed photographs atop the piano stared back at her.

Pictures of her grandchildren were among her mother's most valued possessions that she displayed proudly. Pictures were *another* tradition. Pam marveled at how her children had changed through the years. She chuckled at the grandchildren's group shot taken last year: Five Pilgrims and Five Indians. *But there should be one more,* Pam thought. Tears stung her eyes. *My child would be the oldest grandchild. But no one knows my child is missing. My child never had a name. Why didn't I tell anyone?*

I'm the only one who knows the combination to the safe that hides my secret. Should I open the door and tell my family? What would they think now? Or should I keep my secret locked away?

Then Pam saw an empty wooden picture frame on the piano. She picked it up and held it for awhile, then sat it down again. *I wonder what my child would look like. Would he have my eyes? In time, maybe I'll share my secret. For now, I'll just tuck my secret back and silently remember him every time I look at the empty frame.*

Sometimes in your grief journey you may suffer in secret. Did you keep your pregnancy a secret because you were afraid or unsure? Maybe you thought it wasn't a big deal if you lost your child in the first few weeks. Or was it too painful to share about your loss because it made you feel like a failure? Even if others do know about your loss, at times they may forget to acknowledge your child or include him in the "count" of children or grandchildren.

If you talk about your child openly, do others act or feel uncomfortable? Maybe that's why you've chosen to be silent. But your heart yearns to speak your child's name, if your child had one. So what if your child is nameless? It's never too late to give a name. I named each of the children I miscarried, sometimes years after the actual loss occurred.

Even though I was unsure about the gender, I sensed they were boys. Naming my children helped me to validate them as individuals and to relieve some of my pain and uncertainty about their identity. Although some people raise their eyebrows when I call the children I lost by name, framing their existence in a name helps me to honor them and relate to them, even if I never knew them.

How have you been suffering in secret? What are you hiding in the safe behind the picture of your life? God knows the combination to your personal safe. Maybe it's time to let Him open the door to expose the secret suffering of your loss. Is there an empty picture frame inside? What does it represent to you? Your child is precious to God, and He knows your child by name, even if you or others do not.

Naming your child may be a healing process for you. You may share it with others or only whisper it to yourself. That's up to you. If you choose not to name your child, that's okay too. What's important is to know that God loves you and is here to journey with you through the secret places of your life. He is all-knowing and will never forget you or the child you lost. You are framed forever in His heart.

God, You know the secrets I have locked away in my heart. I feel as if I can't say my child's name or share my true feelings with others because they won't understand. So I suffer in secret. Sometimes, I try to hide my suffering from You too. But I can't. You know exactly what I'm feeling. Open the door to my loss and help me look inside. Fill the empty picture frame of my loss with Your acceptance and compassion. Amen.

Steps Toward Healing

1. How have you suffered in secret about your loss?
2. What feelings have you locked away?
3. Describe your empty picture frame. How do you feel when you look at it?
4. Naming your child is not necessary, but it is certainly acceptable to God.

If you did not name your child and would like to, do so now.

My Personal Journey

Devotion 9
HAPPY-SAD DAYS

• • •

I the LORD do not change.

MALACHI 3:6

"MOMMY, WHY DO YOU look so sad today?" My young son's question startled me as I glanced at myself in the rearview mirror.

I do look sad, I thought. *But why?* I checked off each item from my mental list:

Hormones

Time of month

Lack of sleep

Caffeine

Anniversary date of my baby's death

Day of the week

"I don't know, Jake," I responded. My answer seemed to appease him, but it sparked my curiosity. I was determined to solve the mystery behind my feelings.

Mood swings, tears, and depression were familiar companions to me since losing my baby. I never knew when they would appear at the doorstep of my emotions, though often a holiday, event, or memory summoned their presence. I recall one Mother's Day at church when all the women who had babies that year were asked to stand. I remained seated, but I wanted to stand and scream, "I had a baby too!"

The day I received free baby products and a coupon for a baby portrait in the mail I erupted into tears. The day of Jake's first-grade open house was a tender time when his teacher showed me his family sketch: three stick figures holding hands in front of a house and two stick figures in the clouds.

Lord, what is triggering my emotions today? I prayed silently. *Help me label my unnamed suffering.* Then it hit me. *It's my due date! I should be in labor today and celebrating the arrival of my precious baby. How could I have forgotten?* Guilt knocked at my heart's door, but I refused to let it in.

Instead, I gave myself permission to think about the child I never knew. *What would he look like? What would his cry sound like? How would it feel to hold him? Would he enjoy his bath? How would he and his brother get along?*

I continued to ponder. *Did he know that I almost forgot about today? Did he know that I loved him and missed him? What was it like for him to be in God's presence and to have no suffering?*

Suddenly I realized that Jake was staring at me. "Mom, why do you look *mostly* happy now?"

"Well, I'm happy today because our baby is in heaven, but I'm sad because he would have been born today!" I could tell by my son's silence that he was pondering my comment as we waited at the red light.

Suddenly Jake shouted, "Mom, it's like being a yellow light . . . you're not red and you're not green, but you're a little of each." Jake squeezed my arm and our eyes locked. Amazingly, God used a child and a traffic signal to reveal the truth and affirm my happy-sad emotions that day.

Maybe it's time for you to review your list of holidays, events, or memories. You may discover that today is significant and you have just cause to feel the way you do. Or today may just be a typical day and you feel deeply for no apparent reason. That's possible too, of course.

Grief *is* a lot like a traffic signal — you never know how long it will last or whether you'll feel happy or sad or somewhere in-between on a certain day. And just when you think you've figured it out, it changes.

Lord, what is triggering my emotions today? Is today a significant day? Some of my memories make me smile and others make me sad. I know that it's okay for me to feel both emotions at the same time. Even though my feelings change frequently like a traffic signal, You never do. Your truth is constant. Every day is significant because You are there. Gently remind me of Your presence in my pain and show me how to make it count for good. Amen.

Steps Toward Healing

1. Take a few moments to reflect on your child. How old would he or she be now? What do you think he or she would be like?
2. Certain dates may trigger happy-sad emotions about your child. Some people may grieve these dates silently, while others find it helpful to express their grief through planting a tree or giving to a special cause in memory of their child. What is your plan?
3. Write a letter to your child in heaven. Ask questions. Share your feelings.

MY PERSONAL JOURNEY

MY PERSONAL JOURNEY

Devotion 10

HUSBANDS AND WIVES GRIEVE DIFFERENTLY

● ● ●

Blessed are those who mourn, for they will be comforted.

MATTHEW 5:4

HANNAH AND HER HUSBAND, Elkanah, were a godly Israelite couple in the Bible who enjoyed a loving marriage. When Hannah wept over her barrenness, her husband tried his best to comfort her. "Hannah, why are you weeping? Why don't you eat? Why are you downhearted? Don't I mean more to you than ten sons?" (1 Samuel 1:8)

I can only imagine how Hannah must have felt when she heard his words. Although she knew her husband loved her, his words must have cut to the core of her being. Did Hannah feel as if she was standing on one side of the Grand Canyon and her husband was on the other with the chasm of loss between them?

Elkanah was her best friend. She had always been able to talk to him about anything, and he had affirmed her feelings. That's one of the qualities she admired most about him. She didn't expect *him* to say such cold and unfeeling words. Did Hannah look at Elkanah at that moment and see him more as a distant stranger? How empty and alone she must have felt. Disappointment must have overwhelmed her when she realized her handsome prince was really a frog when it came to understanding her feelings. Why couldn't he understand her pain, see through her eyes, and feel the ache in her soul each time she saw a pregnant woman or baby?

How she must have longed for him to wrap his arms around her and say, "Honey, I'm so sorry you're hurting. I feel the same way." Instead he tried to minimize her pain! Did he really believe he could make up for her loss and satisfy all of her desires? Every time he gave her that knowing look in their bedroom, did she feel inadequate and less of a woman? The pain of desiring a child was enough to endure, but now she had to cope with the loss of his understanding too.

Loss often reveals the distance that can exist between two loving people. You and your husband may express sorrow differently. Women tend to talk openly about their pain and cry frequently, while some men appear cold and unfeeling and sometimes spend more time away from home by losing themselves in work.

You may feel as if your husband is uncaring and doesn't understand your grief. Most men cannot talk easily about their pain and may only express grief when alone. Because men don't bond with the unborn baby the same way women do, men usually grieve quicker. I realized this a few days after my third miscarriage when I asked my husband how he felt about the loss of our child. He shrugged his shoulders, gave me his analytical engineer-look, and said, "I don't feel anything. I don't think of our loss as losing a child since I have never seen the child or related to him."

Ouch! His words hurt. For a moment I felt as if Rich was on one side of the Grand Canyon and I was on the other. How we felt about our child and our loss was the chasm separating us. How I longed to remove the distance I felt. I wanted him to understand the emptiness and sorrow I felt. How I wished I could wave my magic wand and transform his understanding to be like mine.

But I couldn't. God created Rich different from me. Rich, like most men, is a competitive problem solver. He sees himself in the role of protector. He experienced the pregnancy through me — that was his only connection to our unborn child. Since most men are result oriented, they may consider a person as someone they can touch and feel, which in most cases may not be an unborn child. "To me it was just a cluster of cells," one father said, "but to her it was a little boy."

Men often seek comfort from their loss through physical intimacy. Physical intimacy can ease a man's emotional pain. Sometimes the bedroom may become a battleground if you do not understand the way your partner grieves. You may view your bedroom as a place where your child was conceived and it may be painful for you. When your husband gives you that knowing look you may be thinking, "You want to do *what?* It's only been a short time since we lost our child!" You may feel as if your husband is being thoughtless and distant, when in reality he is trying to close the emotional gap he is feeling.

Your husband speaks a different grief language than you do. You may need to ask him to translate what comforts him or what he needs. And be prepared to do the same. Often I just need to talk about it, but I don't want him to minimize my pain or try to solve the problem. I've learned to be direct and tell my husband how I need him to support me in my grief. When I say, "I don't need you to solve my problem, I just need you to listen," he is relieved and usually understands.

Your journey through grief is different from your husband's. At times you may be misunderstood and suffer alone. But you are not alone. God is there with you, and He understands your pain and suffering. He knows what you are thinking and feeling before you ever say a word. And He understands your husband, too. He knows how difficult it is for your husband to see you in pain. Ask God to help you see past hurtful comments and actions from a father who has lost a child too and who doesn't know how to solve the problem for his wife.

God, I feel so alone in my suffering. I wish my husband could understand exactly how I feel, but he can't. I know he loves me, but sometimes I look at him as if he's a stranger. His words and actions meant to comfort me only make my pain worse at times. Forgive me for the way I feel and for wrong actions and words I've spoken to him. Be my communicator. Translate my words and actions to my husband. Help me be sensitive to him. Transform my hurt to hope and the distance I feel to a deepened relationship with You. Amen.

Steps Toward Healing

1. God created you and your spouse different and unique. How does each of you express grief differently?
2. How has your loss created distance between you and your spouse? Drawn you closer?
3. Complete the following sentence: "I feel loved and encouraged when ... " Write down all the ways you feel loved and encouraged and ask your spouse to do the same. Now exchange lists and encourage one another during the next week.
4. Grief over the loss of your child will affect your relationship. Some marriages may become weakened from the stress, while others are strengthened by pulling together through adversity. Guard your marriage and seek help from your pastor, another couple who has survived the loss of a child, or a grief counselor. What is your plan?

MY PERSONAL JOURNEY

Questioning: *to cross-examine, doubt, dispute, examine, analyze, inquire*

If there is anything a sufferer needs, it is not an explanation, but a fresh, new look at God.

DON BAKER, *PAIN'S HIDDEN PURPOSE*

Clearly unless the Lord chooses to explain Himself to us, which often He does not, His motivation and purposes are beyond the reach of mortal man.... Many of our questions — especially those that begin with the word *why* — will have to remain unanswered for the time being.

DR. JAMES DOBSON, *WHEN GOD DOESN'T MAKE SENSE*

As you do not know the path of the wind,
or how the body is formed in a mother's womb,
so you cannot understand the work of God,
the Maker of all things.

ECCLESIASTES 11:5

Devotion 11

DROWNING IN THE SEA OF WHY

●—■—●

When you pass through the waters,
I will be with you;
and when you pass through the rivers,
they will not sweep over you.

ISAIAH 43:2

"MOMMY, WHY DO ALL our babies have to die?"

This question still left me speechless, though it was not the first time my son had asked it. Should I respond differently from what I had before to my brokenhearted son, who had prayed fervently for a baby?

At that moment I felt as if I had just been thrown overboard and was drowning in the Sea of Why. I, too, had questions that flooded my mind. Why, after suffering a miscarriage and adopting Jake, did our baby, John Samuel, die? Why, after losing him, did I have two more miscarriages? And why was my son still asking me the same question?

The Sea of Why was massive and encircled me. Waves of wondering crashed against my soul. The undercurrent of uncertainty began to pull me beneath the dark, mysterious surface. I struggled to stay afloat, but it seemed the more I questioned, the deeper I sank into the unknown. *God, please help me!* I prayed. *I don't know what to say to my son this time.*

Suddenly, my spirit buoyed. *That's it!* I thought. I sensed God's answer as He revealed the line of hope that would rescue me. "I still don't know, Jake!" I said as I gazed deep into his eyes. "All I know is that God is there, He is good, and that's enough." I felt relieved to admit once again, "God, I don't understand!"

Often we don't understand the whys of our circumstance. Our questions remain unanswered and we find ourselves flailing in the Sea of Why. What we believe about God during those times of uncertainty will influence how we respond. If we believe that our circumstance is something Satan slipped by God when He wasn't looking, we will plummet to the depths and drown in despair. But if we view the God of the Bible as sovereign, supreme, and the One who calms the waters, we are buoyed with hope. We see purpose, even though we may not know now what the purpose is.

Most of us in the journey of grieving the child we never knew will find ourselves in the Sea of Why, pondering our loss. During times of questioning I reflect on Job's life and remember that God allows suffering and has purpose in our pain. I must choose to look beyond "the why" to "the Who" and view my loss through the lens of God rather than human sight.

Are you drowning in the Sea of Why? God understands. He is there. He is good. Look to Him. Sometimes that's the only answer there is.

God, even though I still don't understand why this has happened and maybe never will, I know that You are unchanging, trustworthy, in control, and good. I believe You have a purpose in what has taken place. Forgive me for asking the same questions. Buoy me up once again with Your hope and truth. As I continue to journey through questioning, rescue me from drowning in despair. Help me trust You with all of my heart and not lean on my own understanding. Give me divine vision and enable me to see beyond "the why" to "the Who." Amen.

Steps Toward Healing

1. What questions remain unanswered about your loss?
2. Are there resources, people, or professionals who may have answers? What steps could you take to seek solutions?

3. Like Job, we may never have our questions answered. How does that make you feel? It's interesting to note in the book of Job that, in response to sixteen "whys," there are fifty-nine "whos," which refer to God.

The next time you ask "why" about your loss, consider changing the "y" in that word to "o."

MY PERSONAL JOURNEY

_____

_____

_____

_____

_____

_____

_____

_____

_____

_____

_____

_____

_____

Devotion 12

WHY AM I SO ANGRY?

• • •

Get rid of all bitterness, rage and anger.

EPHESIANS 4:31

PAUL SLAMMED THE DOOR. Sara knew by the way her husband stomped up the steps from talking to their neighbors that he was angry.

"What's wrong?" she asked.

"Judy's pregnant!" he snapped. "She told me she didn't even want to have a third child. It was an accident."

Sara could see behind her husband's anger to the hurt and disappointment he felt as he blurted out, "We've been trying to have a child for nearly two years and all we have to show for it is temperature charts, ovulation kits, and a positive pregnancy stick before we lost the baby. Why her and not us?"

Jennie thought the family reunion would lift her spirits. This was her first public outing since losing her second stillborn son. The doctor could not determine the cause of death and warned her not to have another child. Plagued with sorrow, she did her best to enjoy conversation, food, and games with her relatives.

Everything was going fine until her sister-in-law approached her with a baby in her arms. She felt as if the dam was about to break on her emotions, though somehow she managed to hold them back until she arrived home. Then she released her floodgate of tears and anger. *Why did I lose*

*my sons? Why was my sister-in-law so insensitive? Why can't I have a baby like
her? If God is so good, why did He allow this to happen to me?* she vented.

For years Jennie made excuses why she avoided her sister-in-law and
didn't like her. Her unanswered stream of questions about her loss were
now a raging river of anger. Unaware that she had allowed her hostility
to build and separate her from others, Jennie finally realized that she
needed to face her dam of anger and discover how she could release it.

Anger is a natural part of your grieving process. Of all the grieving
responses, I believe anger is the most difficult to accept, especially if you
are a Christian. You may feel angry at your spouse who did not give you
support, or at friends for things they said. Perhaps you are mad at other
women who have complication-free pregnancies and give birth to
healthy babies. Or perhaps you are furious at women who have aborted
a child.

Maybe you've shouted at your body, "Why did you let me down?"
You may find you get angry at little things that never used to bother you.
And if you are honest enough to admit it, you might even be angry at
God. Have you ever wanted to scream, "God, You have the power of life
and death. You could have performed a miracle and protected my baby,
yet You didn't! Why?"

For a long time anger scared me. I didn't feel it was an appropriate
response to my pain. It wasn't until a friend challenged me to write a letter to God and share my personal disappointments that I realized how
dammed up my anger had become. As I sat alone in my backyard with
a blank notebook and pen in my hand, I released my floodgate of questions and emotions. Several red-penned pages later, I felt as if the waters
of my life were flowing peacefully.

Since then I've learned that anger is a natural, necessary part of the
journey through grief. Anger is usually a secondary emotion blocking
the real cause of our pain. It may be disguised as rejection, disappointment, unmet expectations, envy, guilt, fear, or a multitude of other pos-
sibilities. When I feel angry I stop and ask myself, Why *am I angry?*
What *is behind the anger that I feel?*

Your journey through anger can be healthy, healing, and righteous. Open the Bible: God, Moses, Job, the authors of the Psalms, the prophets — all demonstrate righteous anger. Jesus Himself overturned the tables of the moneychangers in the temple.

Conflicts between men, women, and God have existed since Adam and Eve ate of the forbidden fruit in the Garden of Eden. So why should you feel so uncomfortable about your anger? When restoration and peace occur in our walk with God, it is often after a floodgate release of anger. In the personal history of many Christians, a holy outburst or revolt has been the first step toward a trusting encounter with God.

Do you or others you know feel angry? If so, that's okay. God created anger and He gives you permission to express yourself in a healthy, righteous way. But *why* are you angry? *What's* behind the anger that you feel? Did someone disappoint you in the way they responded to your loss? Are you envious of others who have what you desire? Are you mad at yourself and feel guilty or afraid? Or do you believe God let you down and rejected your pleas for help?

Maybe it's time to face the anger you've dammed up. Tell God what has disappointed you. Ask Him to show you the truth and real cause behind the dam of anger you have allowed to build. God wants to help you release it and open up the floodgates so that you are restored and the river of your life is flowing peacefully in Him.

> *God, why do I feel so angry? Anger scares me. It makes me feel uncomfortable. What is really behind the anger I feel? Reveal my disappointments. Please show me how to have righteous anger. Break down the dam of anger that I've allowed to separate me from others and from You. Open the floodgates and let the river of Your truth flow through my life so that I am restored and have peace. Amen.*

Steps Toward Healing

1. How have you recently expressed healthy, righteous anger over your loss? Unhealthy anger?
2. What do you feel is behind your anger? Disappointment? Envy? Expectations? Guilt? Physical exhaustion? Fear? Rejection?
3. Tell God how you feel. Write a letter to Him and share your heart.

MY PERSONAL JOURNEY

_____

_____

_____

_____

_____

_____

_____

_____

_____

_____

_____

_____

My Personal Journey

Devotion 13

WHY DO I FEEL SO GUILTY?

• • •

My guilt has overwhelmed me like a burden too heavy to bear.

PSALM 38:4

Come unto me, all you who are weary and burdened, and I will give you rest.

MATTHEW 11:28

AFTER THE BIRTH OF Jesus, King Herod ordered all male children under three years of age in the neighborhood of Bethlehem killed. The Bible says you could hear weeping and mourning throughout the entire city. I'm sure the grieving chorus included parents, grandparents, brothers, sisters, aunts, uncles, cousins, friends, and neighbors.

I can only imagine the gut-wrenching shock and horror the parents must have felt when their precious child was seized from them against their will. *This can't be happening! There must be some mistake! I'll do anything you ask to save my child!* In spite of their protests, pleas, and prayers, they were unable to protect their child. How helpless and anguished these parents felt. *I should have tried harder to save my child. There must have been something I could have done. Why didn't I leave town? I failed.* Did the weight of guilt nearly crush them?

Guilt is one of the most common and intense feelings after the loss of your child. It is a normal part of your grief journey. It is common to wonder if there was something you did to cause this or if you could have prevented your child's death.

You may spend hours going over your actions during your pregnancy or in the days before the baby died. *Did I do everything the doctor said?*

Did I eat right and rest? Was my stress level too high? Were the medications or tests responsible for my loss? Should I have gone to a different doctor or had more tests? Was sexual activity the cause? Would more bed rest have helped?

Don't punish yourself by rewinding and replaying the tape of your life to figure out if you could have done something differently. If the "what ifs" and "if onlys" keep plaguing you for too long, they can damage your self-confidence and your relationships.

Maybe it's time to press "stop" and focus on the One who understands your suffering and can free you from your guilt. Did you know that no suffering can touch you without having first received the permission of God? God is sovereign. He allowed the Bethlehem slayings and He allowed your child to die. As painful as this truth may be to face, sooner or later, you must. No one can fully explain God's actions or plans but God.

As you journey through questioning, remember guilt is not intended to drive you from God, but toward Him. He sees beyond where you are today and will help you press "play" and move forward. Will you let Him today?

God, I feel as if there was something I could have done to save my child. It's hard for me to accept that it's not my fault. I keep replaying the tape of my pregnancy in my mind. Please help me to hit "stop" and look to You. You are the answer. You are sovereign. Nothing can touch my life without Your permission. Free me from my blame. When I feel guilty, remind me to run to You. Help me press "play" today with a new tape and move forward. Amen.

Steps Toward Healing

1. How have you blamed yourself for the loss of your child?
2. Read aloud Isaiah 46:9–10, Matthew 10:29–30, and 2 Chronicles 20:6. God is sovereign. He has supreme authority and power. He controls everything. How does this truth change your perspective?
3. Write the above verses on three-by-five cards. When you sense you are replaying the guilt from your loss, stop...then look at the truth.

MY PERSONAL JOURNEY

_____

_____

_____

_____

_____

_____

_____

_____

_____

_____

_____

_____

_____

Devotion 14

GOD, WHERE ARE YOU?

• • •

Do not be terrified; do not be discouraged, for the LORD your God will be with you wherever you go.

JOSHUA 1:9B

MARTHA LOOKED WORRIED. SHE had never seen her brother, Lazarus, so sick before. He was so weak he could barely walk, and now he was refusing to eat. All of the home remedies she had tried weren't working. And the local doctors just shook their heads. *What more can I do to help him?* she thought.

Then it occurred to her to contact their good friend Jesus. He was a frequent guest in their home and knew Lazarus well. He was known for helping and healing the sick, so much so that one of his nicknames was "the Healer." He would know what to do. Martha sent word to Jesus, requesting his immediate assistance. She felt confident Jesus would come to her aid and heal Lazarus.

She expected Jesus to bound into their home at any moment, but He didn't. *Where are you?* Martha wondered. This wasn't like the Jesus she thought she knew. He was usually quick to respond. She couldn't understand why He hadn't at least acknowledged her request and sent a return message. Martha felt He had abandoned her at a time when she needed Him most. With each passing day, Martha's hopes faded. Finally it was too late. Lazarus died.

Maybe you can relate to Martha. Did you cry out for God to save your child and believe He would? Did you ask Him to come near, but He kept you waiting and wondering? Like Martha, do you feel as if God gave you the silent treatment and didn't respond in the way or in the timing you thought He should have?

When I am on the phone with a friend, I expect her to answer me when I ask her a question. When I wait for a response and hear silence, I begin to wonder if I have been disconnected or if my friend has hung up on me. Silence may mean she is no longer on the line, but it may also mean she is waiting to respond. Sometimes I instinctively know my friend is still on the line even though there is silence. I may not understand the delay or the timing in which she answers me, but she is still on the line and she is still my friend.

When Jesus finally arrived after Lazarus had been dead for four days, Martha confronted Him: "Lord ... if you had been here, my brother would not have died" (John 11:21).

Can you hear the disappointment in her voice? Can you sense the rejection she must have felt? She must have thought He had hung up on her. But He didn't. He was still on the line even if He wasn't physically present. He was waiting to respond until Lazarus was dead so that God could be glorified in a greater way (see John 11:4).

Your journey through grief may lead you through times when you wonder if God is still on the line. *God, where are You?* you ask. But all you hear is silence. Silence can make you feel uncomfortable. You may interpret it to mean that God has abandoned you. But has He really? Just because He hasn't responded in the way and timing that you expected, does that mean He has hung up on you? Maybe He is waiting to respond in His timing and in His way.

You may not like that, but God may have a bigger plan. Perhaps God just wants you to learn to trust Him through the silence. Does He want to reveal Himself to you in a different way? Allow God to communicate to you through His silence. Learn to listen and wait. God says, "Never will I leave you; never will I forsake you" (Hebrews 13:5).

He is a God of truth. He never lies. He hasn't abandoned you or rejected you but is there even if you don't sense He is. He is your Healer and He wants to help you grow to know and trust Him more. Even if you don't hear from Him in the way you desire, He is there — listening, caring, feeling your pain.

> *Lord, where are You? You didn't respond in the way and timing I expected. I feel abandoned and hurt. I feel disconnected and distant from You. Are You listening? Silence makes me feel uncomfortable and rejected. Are You still on the line? Even though I can't see You, I know You are there. You say You will never leave me or forsake me. Please be my Healer. Help me grow and trust You more. I want to know You through the silence. Show me how. Amen.*

Steps Toward Healing

1. How have you experienced God's silence in your grief journey? How does that make you feel?
2. Listen to His words. Read Psalm 4, Matthew 11:28–29, and Luke 6:20–49.
3. Read the story of Lazarus in John 11. Replace Martha's name with yours.

MY PERSONAL JOURNEY

My Personal Journey

JESUS HAS A ROCKING CHAIR

• • •

I waited patiently for the LORD;
he turned to me and heard my cry.
He lifted me out of the slimy pit,
out of the mud and mire;
he set my feet on a rock
and gave me a firm place to stand.
He put a new song in my mouth....

PSALM 40:1—3A

"GOD, AM I SUPPOSED to hurt this much?" I sobbed as I looked at the teddy bear sitting in my rocking chair. "I miss my baby. Where is he now?"

Though often it seemed that God responded to my pleas with silence, that day God answered and encouraged me in an unexpected way. *It's probably another sympathy card,* I thought, as I ripped open the envelope. Although I appreciated receiving cards and letters, today was one of those times in my grief journey when I couldn't concentrate.

I felt relieved when I saw the cassette tape and a hand-scribbled note from my cousin Crystal. Words through song had been Crystal's gift to others since her youth when she and our troop of cousins performed together in homemade matching dresses and 1960s hairstyles as the Homanettes gospel group.

After several years our family ensemble dissolved, but Crystal and her sister Debbie continued music ministry together until Debbie died of cancer. In spite of her pain and loss, Crystal chose to press on and continue singing. Her courage, perseverance, and ability to view her personal difficulties as the bass notes in her life's song inspired me through the years.

Though distance has separated us for most of our lives, God has enabled Crystal and me to stay close in spirit, heart, and prayer. I sensed this tape was one more way God would intertwine our lives.

My curiosity mounted as I slapped the tape into the cassette deck. Music filled the air, but I wasn't expecting what came next. I felt as if Crystal was sitting next to me, singing to my broken heart. Her words rang out, *"He takes the place of Mom and Dad, He's the best parent a child could have....Don't worry about the children, Jesus has a rocking chair...."*

As I pictured my child in the arms of Jesus being rocked back and forth on the heavenly throne, peace penetrated my soul. Though I had never pondered a divine rocking chair before and had no evidence from Scripture that this was true, I did know that God was in control and could do anything, including using these timely lyrics to encourage me.

I sensed God's presence and compassion for me in a personal, powerful way that day. Each time I listen to Crystal's tape, He continues to remind me that He loves and cares about every question I have about my loss. God is my Comforter and continues to use music to soothe my questioning soul.

Maybe it's time you, too, allowed Him to comfort you through music. And while you're listening, why not picture yourself sitting on Jesus' lap. Feel His arms wrap tightly around you as you lay your head on His shoulder. Then He begins to rock ... and rock ... and rock.

Lord, am I supposed to hurt this much? My arms ache to hold and rock my child. I miss my precious baby. Will my life's song always be so sad? Meet me where I am today and encourage me with Your truth. You are my song of hope. It's comforting to imagine that You could be holding my child in Your arms. Right now, I need You to hold me. Wrap Your arms of peace around me and rock away my fears. Put a new song in my mouth. Amen.

Steps Toward Healing

1. How do you feel when you picture Jesus in a rocking chair holding your child? Holding you?
2. What songs have soothed your soul in your grief journey?
3. God affirms music for your grieving soul. Consider the collection of songs and prayers in the book of Psalms. He inspired David and other writers to honestly pour out their hearts, questions, fears, and true feelings. Find truth and comfort there. Read aloud Psalm 16, 17, and 23, or read the psalm that has encouraged you through your pain.
4. Review the list of music resources in the back of this book. Circle the tapes/CDs you have. Listen to these songs today or throughout your journey. If you're ready for a new song, select one from the list and visit a Christian bookstore.

MY PERSONAL JOURNEY

Forgiving: *to pardon or acquit, to cease to feel resentment against*

Forgiveness is the fragrance a violet sheds on the heel that has crushed it.

MARK TWAIN

To forgive is to set a prisoner free and discover the prisoner was you.

AUTHOR UNKNOWN

When somebody you've wronged forgives you, you're spared the dull and self-diminishing throb of a guilty conscience. When you forgive somebody who has wronged you, you're spared the dismal corrosion of bitterness and wounded pride.

FREDERICK BUECHNER

Bear with each other and forgive whatever grievances you may have against one another. Forgive as the Lord forgave you.

COLOSSIANS 3:13

Devotion 16

HIDDEN UNFORGIVENESS

● ● ●

Search me, O God, and know my heart:
test me and know my anxious thoughts.
See if there is any offensive way in me,
and lead me in the way everlasting.

PSALM 139:23—24

"YOUR TEETH LOOK GREAT. No cavities!"

I was surprised by my dentist's words. "Are you sure? Then why is my tooth so sensitive?" I asked. Instinctively I knew *something* was wrong.

My dentist look puzzled. He stared at my x-ray again. "Your tooth looks fine, according to this! But let's take another look. Open wide!"

I cringed when he placed the metal instrument on my tooth. Tap. Tap. Tap. "Ouch!" I screamed.

With a knowing look, my dentist motioned to his assistant. Moments later my face was numb and the sound of a high-pitched drill filled the air. "I found the problem!" he exclaimed.

Hidden beneath my filling was a speck of decay. Although it was too small to detect on an x-ray, it was big enough to irritate the nerve in my tooth. I was relieved. The underlying cause of my pain was finally exposed and could be repaired before greater damage was done. I walked out of the dentist's office with a pain-free smile, renewed hope, and a new filling.

Your journey through grief may feel similar to a toothache at times. You may think you're coping with your loss fine until a person, place, thing, or event triggers a sensitive spot in you. "Ouch," your heart says. Although you try to excuse your outbursts or rationalize your anger, the ache within your soul keeps getting worse. It may even keep you up at night.

When you ask others to diagnose your problem, they're shocked. They think you look great and appear to be handling your loss fine. Instinctively, however, you know *something* is wrong. So you decide to take a deeper look and ask God to help you.

What is causing my pain? you ask. You cringe when He taps on your heart. Memories flood your mind. You recall the person who made thoughtless comments, the unfeeling doctor who did the procedure after your miscarriage, the family member who ignored you, the friend who didn't call to tell you she is expecting, the spouse who wasn't sensitive to your pain.

With a knowing, loving look the Lord softly replies, "Here's the problem — unforgiveness!" Hidden beneath my hurt is a speck of unforgiveness.

Although the resentments, anger, and disappointments I harbor against others seem small, if left undetected and untreated, the decay can destroy me. The underlying cause of my pain is finally exposed and with the Lord's help can be repaired. He holds out his nail-scarred hands and says about his enemies, "Father, forgive them, for they do not know what they are doing" (Luke 23:34).

Have others wounded you with their words or actions? Is it possible that you are holding onto disappointment or resentment toward another person? Maybe it's time to explore what's hidden beneath your hurt. Is there a speck of unforgiveness there?

Invite the Lord to show you whom you need to forgive. Get rid of the decay. Forgive. Ask Him to create a clean heart in you and renew a right spirit within you. Let Him replace your unforgiveness with His filling of love and forgiveness. Then you can press on relieved, restored, and ready to continue your healing journey.

God, I look as if I'm coping with my loss, but sometimes I overact to people and circumstances. That's not like me. I know something is wrong. X-ray my heart and soul. Expose what's hidden there. Do I need to forgive someone? Show me who. Create a clean heart in me and renew a right spirit within me. Fill me with Your love and forgiveness so I can continue my healing journey. Amen.

Steps Toward Healing

1. Have you been sensitive or overreactive to people or situations? If so, how? How is unforgiveness like decay if left untreated?
2. Is there anyone you need to forgive? Who?
3. God will enable you to forgive when you place your confidence in His ability. Read Isaiah 41:10 and Philippians 4:13. Say, "God, thank You for exposing my unforgiveness toward _____. I forgive _____ for _____."

MY PERSONAL JOURNEY

_____

_____

_____

_____

_____

_____

_____

Devotion 17

FORGIVING OTHERS

• • •

Father, forgive them for they do not know what they are doing.

LUKE 23:34

WALT LOOKED AT HIS doctor's diploma hanging on his office wall. *How many babies have I delivered in all these years?* he wondered. Memories of his college days flooded his mind. He chuckled as he recalled his faded pink wardrobe from doing his own laundry and the time he stayed up all night to study for a final and fell asleep during the test.

When he decided to go to medical school on a whim because that's what his roommate was doing, he never dreamed he would make it. And he never imagined how fulfilling his career would be...*I love my job!* He picked up a tiny bib on his desk that said, "Dr. Walt saw me first." Faces of patients flooded his mind...the first-time moms...the woman who was forty-six and thought she had the flu...the twins...the teenagers.

He recalled the poignant moments when he had to share the difficult news to some of his patients. "I'm sorry, you've had a miscarriage." "Your tube has ruptured." "There is no heartbeat!" "Your baby is going to die!" A wave of compassion crashed at his heart as he recalled the look of disbelief in their eyes, the sorrow, the screams, the silence. Walt remembered how helpless he felt as he tried to comfort them. *Doctors are supposed to save lives, not lose them!* he thought. Although he knew he had done everything humanly possible and that some things were out of his control, he still felt disappointed that he couldn't do more.

That's how he felt about Dottie. Just the mention of her name made his eyes fill with tears. She was one of those "special" patients who had touched his life deeply. *She was so excited when I told her she was pregnant with her first child,* he thought. *And when I told her a few weeks later that she had miscarried her child, I'll never forget how devastated she was.*

When Dottie discovered she was pregnant again, Walt was almost as excited as she was. But a few weeks later that changed. His face grew solemn as he recalled the ultrasound report that revealed the rare fatal defect of Dottie's baby. He remembers how angry he felt inside because he couldn't fix her baby. And he was amazed when Dottie told him she would carry her child to term, even though most in her situation would terminate the pregnancy.

Walt talked honestly with Dottie about her forthcoming labor, delivery, and child. He knew he couldn't fully prepare her to hold a dying child. When Elizabeth was born, he was surprised at how Dottie, her friends, and her family lovingly celebrated the birth of this baby. "Dottie and Elizabeth" was the topic of discussion among most of the hospital staff during their brief stay. Walt was surprised at Dottie's inner strength and her insistence that she wanted to take her baby home. What amazed him more was watching more love lavished on Elizabeth during four days than most children receive in a lifetime. He couldn't quite put his finger on it, but he sensed it had something to do with Dottie's God.

It wasn't until years later when Walt accepted God's forgiveness in his own life and was birthed into His kingdom that he realized what a significant role Dottie and Elizabeth had played in his journey to know God personally. Now Walt could understand the source of Dottie's inner strength. He knew that God was more than just a Santa Claus in the sky. He was real and personal to him...the Great Physician, who came to heal the spiritually sick and bind up the brokenhearted, the God who desires to save lives, who wants no one to perish.

God continued to transform Walt's heart. In time he realized that the disappointment, anger, and resentment he felt toward others needed to be released. *I need to forgive others even if I don't agree with their choices,* he thought. And he did (and does) — one patient at a time.

But he also prays silently for his patients and is on call for God — ready to deliver a physical baby or a spiritual one.

I know because I was a recipient of Dr. Walt's prayers, support, and friendship when I walked on the same path that my friend Dottie had trod twelve years earlier. Ironically, I only knew him then as Dr. Walt, Dottie's doctor. But God chose to reconnect our lives through my friend Diane when she announced her surprise engagement. I nearly fainted when I discovered her husband-to-be was Dr. Walt. Only God could have orchestrated this.

I didn't know at the time how significant our friendship would become, but God did. He knew that Dr. Walt would become a vital support to our family and to my doctor during our journey through the valley of the shadow of death. God knew I would ask Dr. Walt to be my back-up delivery doctor if my doctor was out of town when I went into labor. Even though Dr. Walt didn't deliver our child, somehow just knowing that he was willing to and would lovingly welcome our child into the world gave me peace.

Doctors and medical staff play a significant role in your loss experience. Maybe you've been wounded by their bedside manner, insensitive comments, or their minimizing your pain. Or did you have a caring doctor like Dr. Walt? If so, thank God for how He used your doctor.

Three years after the death of my son, my doctor finally shared with me an incident that still haunted him about my loss. "Kathe, do you remember when you had your baby and it was the change of shifts?" he asked.

I nodded.

"I'll never forget the thoughtless comment the new nurse made to you when you were holding your baby. She called your child an 'it' and 'not normal.'" I could see the pain in his eyes as he continued, "I could have died!"

By God's grace, I couldn't recall these words. But my doctor could. Three years later it still hurt for him to talk about it.

"That's just like God, isn't it?" I said to my doctor. "To erase hurts from our hearts and memory." My doctor gave me a funny look as he nodded.

I'll never know fully how my words or actions through my journey of losing a child affected my doctor or others in the medical community. I can only hope that others saw a glimpse of the Great Physician through me and that my life reflected Jesus' word, "Father, forgive them, for they do not know what they are doing."

Are you holding anger or resentment toward your doctor, the medical staff, or others about your loss? Maybe there is just cause, or maybe they did everything they could for you and your baby. Only God knows. Maybe it's time to forgive those who have hurt you.

Whom do you need to forgive? Allow the Great Physician to deliver you from your hurt and to help you release those from your grip of blame. Ask Him to birth a spirit of forgiveness in you and to show it to others.

God, You are the Great Physician. You ordain birth and death. Sometimes I expect too much from others. When I feel they let me down with their actions or comments, I feel anger and resentment toward them. Please show me the people I need to forgive who hurt me when I lost my child. Deliver me from my hurt and help me release my blame. Birth a new spirit of forgiveness in me so I can truly say, "Father, forgive them, for they do not know what they are doing."

Steps Toward Healing

1. Do you blame anyone for your loss or for hurting you through your experience of loss?
2. List those you need to forgive.
3. How do Jesus' words "Father, forgive them for they do not know what they are doing" encourage you to do the same?
4. Write these words in red letters over your list of names. Tear up the paper and throw it away.

MY PERSONAL JOURNEY

Devotion 18

JOURNEY TO THE SNOWDRIFT OF FORGIVING YOURSELF

● ● ●

Set me free from my prison,
that I may praise your name.

PSALM 142:7

KIM ROCKED WITH GRIEF. "Do something! Please do something. Help my baby!" she wailed. The doctors reassured her there was nothing they could do to save her premature child. *This can't be happening,* she thought as she held her miniature son in her arms. *He looks perfect. He even has his daddy's face.* She counted his tiny fingers and his toes. She stroked the hair on his apple-sized head.

She had longed for a son and had been the model patient to maintain this pregnancy and stop the labor. She recalled her doctor's warning that if her baby was born too soon, he would not survive. She never dreamed she would have to face this circumstance. But as she watched her baby gasp for every breath and then lay still, she knew that her worst nightmare had come true. *My child is dead and it's my fault!*

Like Kim, you may blame yourself for the loss of your child. "My body failed me and didn't fulfill its purpose." "If only my hormone levels hadn't dropped." "I didn't go to the hospital soon enough." "I was too active and stressed." "I made a wrong choice."

You may feel as if you're "snowed in" from the winter storm of your grief. The icy winds of your memories blow against the door of your heart. The snow of self-blame keeps falling. Layer upon layer of guilt builds outside the door of your heart until your mound of guilt is so high you wonder if you'll ever be able to dig out. You're trapped. How will you get out?

In the book of Ruth, when Naomi lost her husband and two sons, I wonder if she felt "snowed in" from guilt and in some way responsible for their deaths? Did she heap layers of self-blame against the door of her heart? *If only I had refused to move here, they might still be alive. Because I condoned my sons marrying unbelievers, God is punishing me.*

The wind of her sons' memory must have blown against the door of her heart every time she looked at her daughter-in-law, Ruth. Ruth could have started a new life with the support of her friends and family in her hometown in Moab. Instead, she traded certainty for an unknown future in a foreign land with an old woman.

Even the sound of her name, "Naomi," which meant "pleasant," made her cringe with guilt. "Call me Mara [Mara means bitter]," she said. "... I went away full, but the LORD has brought me back empty" (Ruth 1:20–21).

Naomi's mound of guilt must have been so high outside the door of her heart that she didn't believe she would ever dig out, and it appeared as if she didn't want to. Was Naomi's guilt justified? Only God knows. How could she dig out of her snowdrift of guilt? She didn't know. But God did. He used her relative Boaz, a kinsman-redeemer, to help her.

I can only imagine how Naomi felt when Ruth came home after working in the fields and told Naomi about Boaz's acts of kindness. She must have felt a bit reluctant to trust. Bitterness and self-blame felt more comfortable. Yet in spite of how she may have felt, Boaz continued to provide for Naomi and Ruth. His love and faithfulness may have changed her heart and attitude, or maybe someone she knew confronted her. Did she hear a still, small voice within a whisper, "Naomi, it's time to free yourself from your past and your guilt and forgive yourself"?

I like to think God melted away Naomi's guilt and helped her see her need to trust Him and forgive herself. God replaced her blame with forgiveness and her mourning with joy.

God can do the same for you. Is a still, small voice within calling your name. Listen. Can you hear Him saying, "It's time to free yourself from your guilt and forgive yourself!"

Your grief journey may lead you to a place where you need to forgive yourself. The concept of letting go of anger, guilt, and condemnation toward yourself may be something you have never considered as sin, which keeps you separated from God. God will forgive you and will enable you to forgive yourself. Perhaps you even need to forgive yourself for placing blame needlessly on yourself.

Regardless of your circumstance, God understands. He is able to melt away the snow mound of guilt outside the door of your heart. He is your kinsman-redeemer, the One who offers you love, kindness, and forgiveness. Ask Him to dig through the snowdrift of your guilt and melt away the blame outside the door of your heart. He is ready to restore you so you can journey on.

Lord, I feel so guilty and often blame myself for losing my child. Although others try to comfort and console me, deep down inside I'm haunted by the thought that I could have done more or made different choices. I feel snowed in from my grief. My mound of self-condemnation is so high outside the door of my heart that I feel as if I'll never be able to dig out. Help me, God. Enable me to forgive myself. Dig through the snowdrift of my guilt and melt away my blame. You are my kinsman-redeemer, the One who has the power to set me free. Restore me today. Amen.

Steps Toward Healing

1. How do you feel guilty or blame yourself for the loss of your child?
2. Have you forgiven yourself? If not, maybe it's time to share your feelings with God. Read 1 John 1:9.

3. *Now personalize 1 John 1:9:* I confess my sin of blaming myself for
   _____. God is faithful and just and has forgiven me for my
   sin and purified me from all unrighteousness. I am forgiven!
   Date _____
4. Live forgiven. The next time you are tempted to blame yourself
   for the loss of your child, refer to this page.

MY PERSONAL JOURNEY

_____

_____

_____

_____

_____

_____

_____

_____

_____

_____

_____

_____

_____

_____

Devotion 19

FORGIVING GOD

● ● ●

Why does this fellow talk like that? He's blaspheming! Who can forgive sins but God alone?

MARK 2:7

THERESA WAS NEWLY MARRIED and looking forward to starting a family. She dreamed of becoming a mother. When she discovered she was pregnant, she knew God had answered her prayer, so she threw a party to celebrate. She felt as if life couldn't get any better. But her fairy-tale life turned into a nightmare the day the pain in her side wouldn't subside and she was rushed to the hospital. She prayed that her baby would be safe.

When she woke up in the recovery room, her first question to her husband was, "Is our baby okay?" He squeezed her hand, his eyes filled with tears: "Honey, I'm sorry. We couldn't save the baby. You had a tubal pregnancy. Surgery was necessary or we could have lost you."

At that moment Theresa wished that *she* was dead, not her baby. Over the next several months her grief turned inward. Depression invaded her life. She avoided friends and family. Her appetite and sex drive diminished. Negative thinking and critical words became her new nature. Routine activities like climbing out of bed, dressing, and cooking exhausted her. She snapped at her husband for no apparent reason.

One day Lynne ignored Theresa's excuses and showed up at her home anyway. "Get dressed!" Lynne announced. "We're going for a drive. It's time for you to come out of your cave of hibernation."

An hour later Lynne and Theresa arrived at a lush parklike setting. Her friend got out of the car, opened her trunk, pulled out a red helium balloon, and handed it to Theresa. *What is this for?* Theresa thought, as she followed Lynne to a nearby picnic table and sat down with her floating balloon. They talked for a while. Then Lynne leaned across the table, looked straight into her eyes, and asked, "Have you forgiven God?"

Theresa was stunned. She wasn't expecting *that* question.

"I've learned that there are usually three people we blame when life doesn't go according to our plans," Lynne said. "Ourselves...others...and God. From what you've told me, I don't believe you blame yourself, your husband, or the doctors for losing your child. So that only leaves God."

Theresa was silent. Somehow the thought of forgiving *God* felt wrong. She felt guilty for even entertaining the thought. But the more she pondered the idea of forgiving God, the more she wondered if her friend was right.

Lynne gave Theresa a knowing look as she handed her a thick black marker. "Theresa, take time to be alone with God right now and talk to Him. Tell Him what you're feeling and ask Him to show you if you are angry at Him and need to forgive Him. Write a letter to Him with this marker on your balloon and then release it," Lynne instructed. "And... don't worry, your balloon is environmentally safe!" she chuckled.

Theresa sat alone at the table. She felt uneasy at first talking to God because it had been awhile since she had. She listened and waited. Then she poured out her heart.

"God, You allowed my child to die. All I ever wanted was to be a mom!" she sobbed. She continued to share her hurts with Him until she had nothing more to say. Then she scribbled on her balloon, stood up, and released it. She watched the red ball ascend slowly, growing smaller with every passing minute until she could only see a speck in the sky... then it was gone.

Theresa felt a soothing calm within her soul. She sensed this was a healing moment in her grief journey. Finally, she was at peace with God.

The concept of "forgiving God" makes me feel uneasy. It sounds prideful and self-righteous. Yet anger and bitterness toward God are far more common than most of us would like to admit. If we are honest about our anger toward God and admit how we feel that God has let us down or has been unfair, then we can begin to heal.

Forgiving God doesn't mean He's guilty, because He cannot commit any sin. But we need to destroy "every pretension that sets itself up against the knowledge of God, and…take captive every thought to make it obedient to Christ" (2 Corinthians 10:5).

Our thoughts may be rooted in perceptions of reality rather than in reality itself. When we forgive God, we release our expectations of what we *think* God should have done to prevent hurt, failure, or loss of any kind. God has big shoulders and allows us to vent. He wants us to tell Him how we feel so we can trust again. Satan is defeated when we stop pointing our finger at God and admit our false expectations.

Are you angry at God about your loss? Do you feel as if He let you down and should have intervened to change your situation? Even though God hasn't done anything wrong, do you feel as if you need to forgive Him? God understands. He suffered the loss of a child too.

Take time to talk to Him. Tell Him how you hurt. You, too, can grab a helium balloon and a marker if you want and write Him a note on the balloon, describing the ways you feel He let you down. Now release it. Go ahead, let it go! Watch your unmet expectations float skyward until they disappear. Allow God's peace to soothe you as you continue to heal in your journey through grief.

> *God, I feel You let me down. I'm hurt, disappointed, and angry at You for _____. Please forgive me for thinking that I need to forgive You. You are sinless and perfect. Help me release to You my unmet expectations so that I can continue to heal. Amen.*

Steps Toward Healing

1. Forgiving yourself and others seems natural, *but forgiving God?* How does that concept make you feel?
2. Do you at times feel as if God let you down? In what ways? Tell Him.
3. Take a thick marker and a helium balloon. Write on it the ways you feel God has let you down.
4. Ask God to help you release your balloon.

MY PERSONAL JOURNEY

_____

_____

_____

_____

_____

_____

_____

_____

_____

_____

_____

_____

_____

_____

_____

Devotion 20

RECEIVING THE GIFT OF
FORGIVENESS

● ● ●

*For God so loved the world that he gave his one and only Son, that whoever
believes in him shall not perish but have eternal life.*

Everyone who believes in him [Jesus] receives forgiveness of sins through his name.

ACTS 10:43

GIFT GIVING IS A fun Christmas tradition that our family enjoys. As a child, I remember running to the Christmas tree to search for packages that seemed magically to appear. I was elated one Christmas morning when I discovered the oversized box was for *me*. I can still recall squealing with excitement when I looked inside and realized the brown fluff of fur with the big red bow was a puppy. At the time, I didn't fully comprehend or appreciate how my gift was provided. However, now I realize that gift giving has three essential elements: the Giver, the Gift, and the Receiver.

The Giver chooses and gives the gift. Motivated by an attitude of love or concern for the receiver, the giver's greatest desire is to know the receiver and give a meaningful, personal gift. That's what my parents did when they gave me a puppy. They selected a personal gift for me that they knew I had longed for.

The Gift comes at some cost or sacrifice to the giver and is free and unearned to those who receive it. My parents sacrificed time, money, trips to the vet, and sleep to give me a puppy.

The gift-giving process is finally complete when *the Receiver* accepts the gift into her possession. Only then does she receive the benefit of the giver's gift. I eagerly received my puppy with enthusiasm and joy!

Gifts, like puppies, come in all shapes and sizes. Most gifts are tangible, but some are not. Have you ever considered *forgiveness* as a gift? Pardoning or excusing others for wrongdoings and ceasing to feel resentment or anger toward another may be just what you need to do in your journey through grief.

Forgiveness may come wrapped in a variety of ways from different givers. One package may be from your spouse. It may come in the form of tears, an embrace, or "I accept your apology" after you hurled unkind words at him. Another package may contain a call, a card, or an invitation to have lunch from a friend or family member you ignored during the dark days of your loss.

Tucked beneath the tree of your relationships may even be a package from the child you lost. *Do I need forgiveness from my child?* you ask. Your child was a person too. If you feel you let your child down in some way, ask your child to forgive you. Although the contents of this package are void of actions or a response like the others, when you acknowledge you are sorry for the part you feel you played in your child's loss, you sense healing.

I admit that *giving* forgiveness is easier for me than receiving it. Maybe it's because *receiving* implies that *I* am guilty. *I am* the one who hurt or disappointed another person, and I need to make amends for the wrong that I have done.

Some people may refuse to receive your gift of forgiveness. If you have made every attempt to make amends, realize there may be nothing more you can do. You can't control how people respond, so don't try. Focus on what you can control. Take responsibility for your actions, your attitude, and your response to others. Leave the rest up to God. He can soften even the most hardhearted person.

Although your gifts of forgiveness from others will be packaged differently from mine, one shiny black gift with a big red bow marked "From God" is common to both of us and to every person who lives. God's motive in offering us this gift is pure, unconditional love for us.

The gift He offers is free, unearned, and undeserved. It doesn't matter who you are, what you've done, or where you came from, God wants to give you a personal gift because He cares.

This shiny black package reminds us of how we "all have sinned and fall short of the glory of God" (Romans 3:23). Our sin and wrongdoings separate us from God. The big red bow reminds us that God's gift was made with great love and sacrifice: "For God so loved the world that He gave his one and only Son, that whoever believes in him shall not perish but have eternal life." Jesus died on the cross for your sins and mine, and He rose again so that we can live with God forever.

Have you received God's gift of eternal life and his forgiveness by believing in Jesus? If so, thank Him for this gift. If not, maybe it's time. God wants you to have this gift. He loves you so much. Go ahead, accept it.

When you do, lift the lid off the box and look inside. It's white and empty. That's the way God sees you now — clean, without sin, forgiven. He will help you keep it that way — one situation and one person at a time.

Why not start right now. Ask Him to help you see whom you have wronged, then ask for forgiveness. Forgiveness is a gift for you to receive from God and from others. Why not pass on the tradition to someone else?

God, thank You for reminding me that giving and receiving forgiveness is a necessary part of my healing journey. Tucked beneath the tree of my relationships are people I have hurt. From whom do I need to receive the gift of forgiveness? Please forgive me for how my thoughts, words, and actions have wounded others. My expectations and conditional love got in the way. Give me courage to tell others "I'm sorry" and ask them to forgive me. Remind me each time I look at a Christmas gift that You gave me an oversized gift I didn't deserve — Your life. Thank You for wrapping Yourself around my sins and for willingly dying on a cross for me. Your bow of sacrifice demonstrates Your unconditional love for me. I accept Your gift. Give me courage to admit my wrong to others and to receive their gift of forgiveness too. Amen.

Steps Toward Healing

1. What was your favorite Christmas gift as a child? How did you feel when you opened it?
2. Do you most enjoy giving gifts or receiving them? Why?
3. Is it easier for you to give forgiveness or receive it? Why?
4. Think about God's gift of forgiveness wrapped up under the tree of eternal life. The tag has your name on it. To: _____ From: <u>God</u>. What draws you to open it? What makes you reluctant to accept it?
5. Whom have you hurt with your words, thoughts, or actions and from whom do you need to ask for the gift of forgiveness? To: _____ From:_____ Tell them. Give them the gift of "I'm sorry, will you please forgive me?" and receive the gift from them.

MY PERSONAL JOURNEY

_____
_____
_____
_____
_____
_____
_____

RELATING

Relating: *to tell, show, establish a logical or casual association, connect with*

● ● ●

What Do You Say...

What do you say when a baby dies and someone says...
"At least you didn't bring it home."
What do you say when a baby is stillborn and someone says...
"At least it never lived."
What do you say when a mother of three says...
"Think of all the time you'll have."
What do you say when so many say...
"You can always have another."
What do you say when someone says...nothing?
What do you say when someone says..."I'm sorry."
You say, with grateful tears and warm embrace,
"Thank you!"

REPRINTED WITH PERMISSION OF BEREAVEMENT SERVICES,
GUNDERSEN LUTHERAN MEDICAL FOUNDATION, LACROSSE, WISCONSIN

We all need "Kleenex & candle" friends when we suffer loss. Compassionate companions who give us permission to cry and offer a Kleenex or their tears. When the darkness of discouragement comes they encircle us. Our heroes of hope light the way to brighter tomorrows and to the One who is truth and our eternal encouragement. And at the right season, we can pass on what we have received to others...a Kleenex & a candle.

KATHE WUNNENBERG

Devotion 21

WHO DO YOU SAY THAT I AM?

• • •

[Jesus] asked his disciples, "Who do people say the Son of Man is?"
They replied, "Some say John the Baptist; others say Elijah; and still others,
Jeremiah or one of the prophets."
"But what about you?" he asked. "Who do you say I am?"
Simon Peter answered, "You are the Christ, the Son of the living God."

MATTHEW 16:13B—16

"HOW MANY CHILDREN DO you have?" the waiter asked as he handed me the menu.

His question startled me. *How should I respond?* I wondered. Before I could say a word, however, my nine-year-old son, Jake, said with confidence, "Six! Four in heaven and two on earth!" I don't know who was more surprised — me, my husband, or the waiter.

As you journey through grief, you may find yourself in unexpected situations where you need to communicate your loss with others. Like ordering from a menu at a restaurant, you have a multitude of options from which to choose. The depth of your sharing about your loss is up to you. You may choose to share little, much, or not at all. Your decision may depend on the circumstances or the people involved in each encounter.

When Jesus asked His disciples, "Who do people say the Son of Man is?" I wonder if they felt caught off guard and awkward. How should they respond to Jesus? Their responses were varied.

"Some say John the Baptist; others say Elijah; and still others, Jeremiah or one of the prophets."

Jesus went on to ask them, "But what about you? Who do you say that I am?"

Simon Peter replied, "You are the Christ, the Son of the living God."

I can sense the confidence in the way Peter proclaimed his answer. Without hesitation he spoke. Did Peter anticipate being asked this question? Did he predetermine what he would say? Although the Bible doesn't tell us, I think it's safe to assume that Peter was comfortable with his response and spoke honestly. He shared the truth.

I have discovered that it is helpful to anticipate the situations where you may be asked pointed questions and preplan your response. What will you say? How much will you share? With whom will you share? How will you refer to your child? How will you refer to yourself? Do you know what your husband or children will say about your loss?

Advance planning can prevent hurt feelings or awkward moments. Feeling comfortable with words that describe your child or loss experience can help you relate your loss to others in a positive and healthy way. Communication can be a healing part of your journey through grief.

Who do you say that you are since you've lost a child? Are you still a mother even though you have empty arms? Are you a mother of one, two, three, or more?

Who do you say your child is? A baby, "it," "nature's way of ending something that shouldn't have been," or a gift from God? That's a question only you can answer and relate to others.

And who do you say Jesus is? How you respond to this question has eternal consequences. Like Peter, I hope you say with confidence, "You are the Christ, the Son of the living God."

God, how should I communicate my loss to others? Sometimes I feel uncomfortable and tongue-tied. I want to speak with ease. Please show me how. Guide my words with Your wisdom. Prepare me to respond to others. Who do You say that I am? Thank You for being my Father and for sending Your Son Jesus to die for me. I can say with confidence I will spend eternity with You as Your child. Amen.

Steps Toward Healing

1. How has loss changed you?
2. What new insights has God shown you about yourself?
3. Who do you say that you are? How can you express that to others?
4. You will always be a child of God regardless of the changes in your life. How does that make you feel? How does your experience of loss give you new opportunities to share your identity in Him with others?

MY PERSONAL JOURNEY

_____
_____
_____
_____
_____
_____
_____
_____
_____
_____

Devotion 22

HE'LL MEET YOU WHERE YOU ARE

● ● ●

Are not two sparrows sold for a penny? Yet not one of them will fall to the ground apart from the will of your Father. And even the very hairs of your head are all numbered. So don't be afraid; you are worth more than many sparrows.

MATTHEW 10:29–31

"KATH, COME QUICK!"

I knew BY THE TONE OF MY HUSBAND'S VOICE THAT SOMETHING WAS TERRIBLY WRONG AS I WADDLED THROUGH THE BACKYARD TOWARD HIM AND JAKE, OUR SIX-YEAR-OLD SON.

"It's a baby bird!" sobbed Jake, as he knelt on the ground beneath the ladder.

I stepped closer and then I saw the spoon-sized, featherless creature lying next to a clump of twigs.

My husband's eyes dimmed with disappointment. "I had no idea a baby bird was in the nest!" he said.

Jake looked up at me. Tears streamed down his face. "Mom, can we save him?"

How I longed to tell my son at that moment what he desired to hear, that I could miraculously heal this baby bird — but I could not. As traumatic as this moment was, I knew I must tell him the truth. "No, Jake, I'm sorry. The baby bird is dead," I solemnly replied. Then I knelt down, wrapped my arms around my son, and cried with him.

The baby bird was Jake's first personal encounter with death. I couldn't minimize this experience or the pain he was feeling, so I met him where he was and joined him in his grief encounter. Together, our family buried the baby bird and thanked God for its brief life. Ironically, three weeks later, we stood together once again, but this time at a cemetery, where we thanked God for the brief life of our child.

Was this a coincidence or was this God's way of meeting us where we were to relate to us? I'll never know for sure in this lifetime, but I do know that Jesus is a relational expert. He touches people where they are and communicates to them in a unique way they can understand. He met the woman at the well at midday because He knew that's when a woman with her reputation would be there. James and John were working by the seashore when Jesus met them and invited them to become "fishers of men." He hung between two criminals, one of whom accepted His offer to join Him in Paradise.

Encounters with Jesus were often simple, ordinary moments, when He shared about a farmer sowing seeds, sheep, goats, and a vine and its branches. His actions and words met listeners where they were and related truth in a way they could understand and apply.

His words still do that. Maybe that's why God chose to use a baby bird to relate death to Jake and prepare him for losing his baby brother. God met him where he was and communicated truth to him in a powerful, meaningful way.

How we choose to relate our loss to others is personal and unique for each of us. I've discovered that honest communication works best in our family. We give each other permission to be where we are in our grief journey, which may mean handing a tissue to the one in tears or having a picnic on a grave. It may mean enduring silence or words, anger or laughter.

Sometimes we choose to celebrate and honor the children we have lost through special ornaments on our Christmas tree, scholarships for needy children, anonymous gifts to families in crisis, sharing our story with others, or giving yellow rubber ducks as baby gifts to others. Though others aren't usually aware of the significance of the duck they've received, I am. It reminds me of the baby bird God used to touch our hearts and helped prepare us for the loss of our child. It prompts me to thank God for relating to me in a personal, meaningful way and encourages me to do the same with others. God continues to meet me where I am. He will do the same for you.

Precious Lord, thank You for demonstrating Your love for me in specific ways and for being my Companion through my hiding, suffering, and questioning. You are the One who knows when every bird falls to the ground. You know the number of hairs on my head. You care about me personally and meet me where I am. Continue to guide me and be my Companion as I journey through relating to others. Amen.

Steps Toward Healing

1. What specific situation or person has God used to meet you in your grief? What did you learn? Why was this encounter meaningful?
2. Think about the people Jesus encountered in the books of Matthew, Mark, Luke, and John. Which person or story can you relate to? Why?
3. If you could honor or celebrate the child you never knew, what would you do? How could you include your circle of family or friends?

My Personal Journey

Devotion 23

JOURNEY THROUGH THE SEASONS
OF FRIENDSHIP

• • •

He is like a tree planted by streams of water, which yields its fruit in season.

PSALM 1:3

I LOVE TREES! THEY refresh me and soothe my soul. They provide shade from the heat, shelter from the rain, and a place to hide, climb, or build a tree house. When transition is thrust on them through the seasons, they adapt. Trees mature in summer and change colors and drop leaves in fall. They know when to shut down to survive winter and when to sprout new beginnings in springtime. Some trees, like the sequoias in northern California, grow in clusters. Their roots web together, enabling them to withstand strong, blustery winds.

Like trees, you will need to endure different seasons in your grief. There will be times when you will need to be rooted in a support system of relationships.

Often through the years and in my grief journey I have felt guilty and uncaring about not maintaining friendships the way I thought I should. My list of expectations included remembering birthdays, meeting regularly, sharing meaningful conversation, and writing or calling often.

I was freed from my slavery of expectations when I heard a friend share about the seasons of friendship. She told me that it is normal to have different friendships through different seasons of one's life. Some are with you through childhood, singleness, and college. Others come alongside of you when you start your career, marriage, or family. Some friends spend a season with you to help you grow spiritually or support you through a change or crisis. And some are friends with you through your grief.

That's how God used Dottie in my life — to mentor me and be a friend through my season of loss and grief. Several years ago, I walked through Dottie's miscarriage and her baby's death. Throughout the months of her pregnancy and through the birth and death of her daughter, Elizabeth, our friendship grew.

A move separated us. Our friendship entered the winter season and was "shut down," but I always felt a kindred spirit with Dottie. Years later when I discovered that my baby would die with the same birth defect as hers, I knew I could make it through because she had. Her friendship had given me courage.

When we reconnected after my son's death, I felt as if we were experiencing springtime in our friendship. She shared new insights about grief with me and what to expect in my months and years ahead. She empathized with my fear of having another child. She is praying for me as I write this book. Only God knows how many seasons Dottie and I will journey on as friends. For now, God has connected us through our grief, and I am grateful.

Jesus wants us to make the most of our seasons of friendship. He met people in the season of life when they needed Him most. Picture the paralytic, the leper, the blind man. The twelve disciples needed Jesus' friendship to teach them, and Jesus knew they would need each other's.

Jesus is your caring, faithful friend during this season of your life when you need Him most. He will never leave you nor forsake you and will be your friend for all seasons. He has provided others to support you during this time in your life. Your "Jesus-with-skin-on" friends understand your pain and are tangible reminders of His love and concern for you. In time, you'll be able to support others who need a friend for a season. Stay close to Jesus. He will guide you.

God, thank You for the gift of my friends and for the seasons of friend-ship with them. Sometimes You place a person in the springtime of my life when I need a new perspective. Or You use them to help me grow and mature. When I need to change or let go, my autumn friends are there for me. And some friends allow me to shut down and be still in the winter of my grieving. They know when to release the friendship. Thank You for draw-ing close to me in the seasons of my grieving. You have been a friend throughout my grief journey. Direct me to those who need a friend for a sea-son in their grief. Amen.

Steps Toward Healing

1. If you don't have any friends for this season of grief, ask God to connect you to someone.
2. Who are the friends who understand your personal experience and grief and are with you in the journey? Which friends:
   - Give you new perspectives?
   - Help you grow and mature?
   - Support you through change?
   - Encourage you to "shut down" and be still?
3. To whom can you be a friend through her season of grieving? Ask God to show you someone you can invest in for a season.
4. God is a friend for all seasons. How do you most need Him to help you this week? To give you new perspectives? To help you grow and mature? To support you through change? To encour-age you to "shut down" and be still?

My Personal Journey

_____

_____

_____

_____

_____

_____

_____

_____

_____

_____

_____

_____

_____

_____

_____

_____

_____

_____

_____

_____

_____

_____

_____

_____

_____

Devotion 24

PLAYMATES IN HEAVEN

- - -

Love one another. As I have loved you, so you must love one another.

JOHN 13:34

GOD OFTEN WILL BRING people across your path who can relate to your loss.

Little did I know that God would answer my prayers to fill the house next door with a friend who understood my broken heart. Just weeks after our baby's death, we saw a family walk out of the house next door. *Could this be our new neighbors?* I wondered. We smiled and waved. They smiled and waved back. "Are you interested in the house?" we asked.

They nodded and walked closer. We told them that the best part of buying the house was to have us as neighbors! We all laughed. Then I noticed their two-year-old daughter and a small white bundle in the woman's arms. "How old is your baby?" I asked.

"Three months," she replied.

What a coincidence, I thought. *Our baby would be two months old.*

A few days later we saw the "Sold" sign. The young family we met would indeed be our new neighbors. Stephanie, the mother, was just the person I needed for this season of my life. She had experienced the death of an infant son a year earlier. His name was Jacob, our living son's name.

God knew exactly what He was doing by connecting our lives. How comforting to have a friend next door who understands my joy, my sorrow, and my journey through grief. On my son John Samuel's birthday I can always count on a card, a hug, or a gift from Stephanie. It means so much to know *someone* remembers. Two days later, it's her son Jacob's birthday and it's my turn to reciprocate.

One year I suggested we go to a lake to commemorate Jacob's life. We sang happy birthday, and then she and her children released balloons and threw flowers in the lake. As her children frolicked by the water, I sat across from Stephanie at a picnic table and listened to her pour out her mother heart. I understood her sorrow and her joy.

"Maybe our boys are playmates in heaven!" I said.

We both smiled at the thought of our sons running through the streets of gold, hearing stories about the Flood from Noah himself, and sitting side by side with Jesus.

Even though I don't know for sure, it's a comforting thought. What I do know is that God is sovereign and is the divine Connector. He intertwined my life with Stephanie's at a time in my grief journey when I needed someone to relate to and who understood my mother heart.

Connecting with others who understand your loss can provide healing in your journey. You may receive encouragement or you may give it. Do you know someone who has also lost a child? If not, ask God to connect you to someone. He wants us to encourage one another in our journey through grief. Maybe your child and mine are playmates in heaven. Only God knows. But one day, we too will know for sure.

God, You are the divine Connector. You have a purpose and plan for the people You have placed in my life. Thank You for caring about me and for others who care too. Help me to be sensitive to others who have lost a child and encourage them. Lead me to those You want me to meet. Amen.

Steps Toward Healing

1. Read 2 Corinthians 1:3–4; Galatians 6:2; Ephesians 4:32; 1 Thessalonians 4:18.
2. How does God want you to respond to others who are grieving?
3. Who has lost a child and would appreciate your encouragement? How will you do this?

Due dates, birthdays, anniversaries, Mother's Day, and Father's Day can be painful days for those who have lost a child. Consider ways you can show comfort to others on those occasions.

MY PERSONAL JOURNEY

_____

_____

_____

_____

_____

_____

_____

_____

_____

_____

_____

_____

_____

Devotion 25

IT'S PITCHER-FILLING TIME!

● ● ●

May the God of hope fill you with all joy and peace as you trust in him, so that you may overflow with hope by the power of the Holy Spirit.

ROMANS 15:13

THE EXPERIENCE OF LOSS can drain the energy from your life and leave you feeling so empty that you are unable to relate to others in a positive way. *I have nothing left to give,* you think. And in most cases, you're probably right.

I've encountered several times in my grief journey like this. Meeting the needs of others comes naturally for me, so when I was unable to do this with joy on one specific occasion, I knew I needed help. I went through my checklist: Am I eating properly? Am I getting enough rest? Are hormones an issue? Do I have too much activity in my life? Is exercise a part of my regular routine? I even explored the possibility of hidden unforgiveness, anger, guilt, sin, and the time of year. (Often I feel drained around the anniversary dates when I lost my children.) I sought medical attention and my physical examination resulted in a healthy, normal report.

Ironically, it was my friend Patty Berens who helped me solve my problem. I was at her workshop, "Learn to Unwind Before You Unravel." Patty picked up a pitcher filled with water and began to pour it into several glasses. She compared this to how we pour out our lives to others each day: our families, job, friends in crisis, and activities. Sooner or later we are dry. *This is exactly how I feel!* I thought.

Then Patty asked, "What are you doing to *fill* your pitcher so you can continue to pour out your life to others?"

Fill my pitcher? I had never considered that before. After all, I'm a "doer." I like to encourage others, but taking time to fill *my* emotional pitcher with people, places, or things that energized *me* seemed selfish. *Was Patty right?*

Since I'm the type of person who has to learn through experience, I decided to try what she suggested. I went home and made a list of "pitcher-filling" items: reading a book, conversation with a friend, pine trees and snow, a manicure, having the night off as "Mom," dining out with my husband, drinking a mocha, going to a bookstore, getting away for a weekend, and having time alone with God.

Then I determined I would fill my pitcher for a week by spending time alone with God and a few other items that energized me. By the end of the week I was amazed at how much better I felt. I was able to laugh again and serve others with a smile. Others noticed my change too and wondered what had happened. "I filled my pitcher!" I answered.

Self-care is important in your journey through grief. Although losing a child may be a onetime event, your loss has a ripple effect on your life that can last a lifetime. Just when you think you are doing great, a situation or person may trigger a painful memory of losing your child and you feel as if your emotional pitcher is being drained.

Be gentle with yourself through the process. If you feel drained of energy and can't find a reason why, is it possible that you've been pouring out so much to others that your emotional pitcher is empty and needs to be filled? Have you neglected spending time with God so that He can fill your spiritual pitcher?

God wants you to live life "to the full" so that you can serve others cheerfully. But He also wants you to love yourself as much as others and take time for self-care. Even Jesus knew His limits and when to stop in order to fill His pitcher. He took time to play, laugh, fish, sleep, and spend time alone with God. He kept pouring out His life for others, but He was able to do that because He knew when and how to keep His pitcher full.

What about you? Have you been pouring out to others so much that you've neglected yourself? Has your loss required you to pour out emotionally even more? Are you drained spiritually and need to be filled? Maybe it's time to fill *your* pitcher. Do something this week that will energize you emotionally. Spend time with God and ask Him to fill you spiritually. He wants you to live energized and to the full. Ask Him to show you how.

God, I'm drained. I feel as if my pitcher is dry and I have nothing left to give to others. Help me love myself and take time for self-care. Show me specific ways that I can fill my emotional pitcher. Draw me close to You and fill me spiritually. It's pitcher-filling time, Lord. Fill me up with Your love so I can pour it out to others. Amen.

Steps Toward Healing

1. How are you pouring out to others daily?
2. God tells us to love our neighbors as ourselves. How are you demonstrating self-love?
3. How do you know if your emotional pitcher is empty?
4. Make a list of specific ways that you or others can fill your pitcher.

MY PERSONAL JOURNEY

SEEKING

Seeking: *to search for, request, aim, or try*

Sorrow looks back,
Worry looks around,
Faith looks up.

AUTHOR UNKNOWN

Ask and it will be given to you; seek and you will find; knock and
the door will be opened to you.

MATTHEW 7:7

Seek God in your darkness and He will be your light.
Seek God in your questions and He will be your answer.
Seek God in your anger and He will be your peace.
Seek God in your sorrow and He will be your comforter.
Seek God in your uncertainty and He will be your confidence.
Seek God in your sin and He will be your redeemer.
Seek God in your forgiveness and He will be your salvation.
Seek God in your salvation and He will be your eternity.

KATHE WUNNENBERG

Devotion 26

SEEING BEYOND YOUR CLOUD
OF LOSS

● ● ●

*"For I know the plans I have for you," declares the Lord, "plans to prosper you
and not to harm you, plans to give you hope and a future. Then you will call
upon me and come and pray to me, and I will listen to you. You will seek me
and find me when you seek me with all your heart. I will be found by you,"
declares the Lord.*

JEREMIAH 29:11–14A

"LOOK UP! WHAT DO you see?" I asked as I pointed to the puffs of white
landscaped across the turquoise sky.

"An elephant! A submarine!" squealed my son Jake. "Mom, look at
that whale! Dad, what do *you* see?"

Silence pervaded the car. I sensed my engineer-minded husband was
not in the mood to play "name that cloud" for the next hundred miles of
our trip.

Jake persisted. "Come on, Dad..."

Finally, Rich responded. "I don't see anything — but clouds!"

Clouds fascinate me. Unlike my husband, I love to watch them
mutate and imagine what they might become. When I look up, I see
beyond a mass of water or ice particles that appears as floating mist or
fog, to a theater in the sky. The blue backdrop sets the stage for the
clouds of changing cast and props.

How we view our loss is a lot like looking at clouds. We may only see
the floating fog of sorrow, or we can choose to look beyond it to a future
in the process of being shaped. Eventually we reach a point in our grief
journey when we must decide whether or not we will allow God to
transform our lives through loss. He knows the plans He has for us, to

give us hope and a future. He knows what He will show us. But first we must look up and trust God wholeheartedly with our uncertainty.

I remember the day I made that decision. Our family and friends had gathered to praise God for the brief life of our son. As I stared at the teddy bear with three helium balloons sitting on the altar, I thought about my child, the plans, and future I would never experience with him in this lifetime. I would never see him take his first step, crash on his bike, play catch with his brother, drive his first car, graduate from high school, marry, or have a child of his own. My plans to read books to him, sing lullabies, and teach him to pray would never come to pass. Would I allow this cloud of loss to cast a shadow on the rest of my life? I knew that was a decision only I could make. *But how do I see beyond it?* I wondered.

We gave helium balloons to each of our guests to release as they left. I decided to cling to mine as I walked outside. Then I looked up. Clouds were everywhere. *They're beautiful!* I thought. At that moment, I sensed God telling me to let go of my loss, so I released my balloon. As I watched it ascend toward the clouds, I felt my spirit lifting and hope returning to me. I knew God had plans for my future and would help me see beyond my cloud of loss. I did not know at the time that He would transform my loss into this book, but He did.

When Christ died, the cloud of loss must have overshadowed the disciples. Did they feel as if their hopes, plans, and future had been erased? Would they ever see beyond the tomb? I can only imagine the hurt and hopelessness they must have felt. Disappointment must have dimmed their view. But three days later, Christ rose from the grave. He defeated death. He transformed their cloud of loss into a future with hope. Did their spirits soar as they looked up and watched Jesus ascend into the clouds to join His Father in heaven?

Someday, when we least expect it, Jesus will come back. I wonder how it will feel on that day to look up at the theater in the sky and see Jesus, center stage, riding on his chariot of clouds.

Maybe it's time for you to look up and invite Him to help you see beyond your loss. He is the Alpha and Omega, the One who is, who was, and who is to come. He knows the plans He has for you, to give you hope beyond your hurt and a future beyond your past. Why not ask Him today? Release your cloud of loss to Him and watch Him begin to transform your life.

God, thank You for clouds. They remind me that You are in the process of shaping my future. Help me to trust You wholeheartedly and see beyond my loss to the plans You have for me. Transform my hurt into healing, my fear into faith, and my past into a future with hope. I release it to You today. You are the Alpha and Omega, the One who is, who was, and who is to come. Remind me to look up as we journey on. Amen.

Steps Toward Healing

1. Look at the cover of this book. What do you see in the clouds?
2. Jesus is the One who transforms lives. In what area(s) of your life physically, psychologically, socially, or spiritually has He transformed you the most through your loss?
3. In what area do you still need to seek His hope?
4. What plans do you sense God may have for you in the future?
5. Read the verse at the beginning of this devotion and insert your name.

MY PERSONAL JOURNEY

Devotion 27

DO YOU WANT TO GET WELL?

● ● ●

He heals the brokenhearted and binds up their wounds.

PSALM 147:3

"FIRST ONE IN GETS healed!" could have been the motto of the disabled people at the pool of Bethesda. The area was landscaped with many blind, lame, and paralyzed people, each hoping to be restored by the healing waters. The stench of unclean bodies and salve filled the air. Most were beggars lying in the rut of despair with no desire or hope for a better future.

One invalid had been there for thirty-eight years. His problem had apparently become a way of life for him. No one had ever helped him and he had lost hope of ever being healed. Jesus approached him and asked, "Do you want to get well?" (John 5:6).

You would think that the man would have shouted, "Yes!" Instead he responded with excuses. Maybe he was afraid of being healed. Healing would mean a new way of life for him. No more begging. How would he get food? He would have to take care of himself and go to work. Did he feel anxious about change and prefer living in the comfort zone of hopelessness?

"Then Jesus said to him, 'Get up! Pick up your mat and walk.' At once the man was cured. He picked up his mat and walked" (John 5:8–9).

You may feel as if your grief has paralyzed you emotionally or spiritually. No matter how trapped you feel in your infirmities from your loss, God can minister to your deepest needs. Don't let your loss cause you to lose hope for the future. God may have special work for you to do — in spite of your loss or because of it.

- Helen Keller allowed others to see God through her blindness.
- God uses Joni Eareckson Tada's paralysis to help others walk spiritually.
- After her son died, Margie started a support group for mothers who lost a child.
- After two of their triplets died, Mark and Karen have become encouragers to help other couples walk through the paralysis of their loss.

Do you want to get well? This is a question you have to ask yourself. Do you want Jesus to heal the areas in your life where you have been wounded by your loss? Or do you want to keep hiding, suffering, questioning, and blaming? Are you comfortable living with your anger, hurt, or depression, or are you ready to seek restoration for your future?

You may be holding tightly to the things that are paralyzing you spiritually. Is it time to forgive yourself or others? Do you need to invite Jesus to come near? Christ can heal all the areas of our life. But if He does, you'll need to let go of your excuses.

Jesus doesn't accept your excuses or see you as you see yourself — lying in a rut of despair. He sees your potential. Through His grace He will work through your loss in the future. He is reaching out His hand to you. "Do you want to get well?" He asks. "Get up and walk."

Go ahead. Seek His healing. Get up and walk. Embrace your future.

Lord, I've been paralyzed in my grief and am lying in a rut of despair. I'm tired of hiding, suffering, questioning, and blaming. I need Your healing. Please forgive me for resisting Your touch. I want to get well! Replace my sorrow with joy, my anger with peace, and my hopelessness with hope. Help me get up and walk into the future. Amen.

Steps Toward Healing

1. Read the story in John 5. Imagine you are the person Jesus approaches and asks, "Do you want to get well?" How will you respond to Him?
2. What excuses have paralyzed you from walking into the future?
3. Maybe it's time to get up and walk into your future! What steps can you take to start?

MY PERSONAL JOURNEY

_____

_____

_____

_____

_____

_____

_____

_____

_____

_____

_____

_____

_____

Devotion 28

HOLDING HANDS WITH
YOUR FUTURE

● ● ●

So do not fear, for I am with you;
do not be dismayed, for I am your God.
I will strengthen you and help you.
I will uphold you with my righteous right hand.

ISAIAH 41:10

WHEN MARK AND KAREN discovered she was expecting triplets, they were surprised and delighted, but also apprehensive. They knew how risky this type of pregnancy could be.

Nineteen weeks into the pregnancy, Karen's water broke and she was rushed to the hospital. Their tiny son, Morgan, was born and within a few hours died.

"You can expect to lose the other two within forty-eight hours," the doctor announced.

Mark and Karen felt as if they were slipping into a hole of hopelessness. Could they climb out of it only to face the future with more loss? Family and friends from coast to coast sought God through prayer. Prayer was the lifeline of hope that pulled them out of their despair. Miraculously, Karen's contractions quit and she began to feel more hopeful that her two remaining babies would be saved. "Don't be too optimistic," the doctor told the couple. "Only a handful of children throughout the world have ever survived a situation like yours!"

"The doctors are only looking at the medical side. They aren't putting God into the equation!" Mark whispered to Karen.

Over the next several days, Karen underwent several medical procedures and finally was sent home on bed rest. Although the doctors thought Mark and Karen were not grasping reality, the couple felt as if God was holding them tightly in the grip of His grace. Friends and family rallied to support them with meals, lawn care, cards, and letters.

Karen felt relieved when Week 25 finally arrived. *My babies can almost survive,* she thought. She wondered what it would feel like in the future when she was able to sit and hold them on the sofa instead of lie on it. *Just a few more weeks...*

But Karen's labor started again, and a week later her doctor performed an emergency C-section. Laura and Sarah were born, each weighing one pound, twelve ounces. Though severely premature, both girls responded well to early treatments. Each day that passed was one day closer to a hopeful future. When they reached the two-week milestone, they knew chances of survival were excellent.

But late one night Mark answered the phone. "Laura is sick. Come immediately!" said the nurse.

Mark and Karen found themselves back on the merry-go-round of emotions, holding tightly to the uncertainty about their future. Would this ride ever stop? During the next several hours Mark and Karen watched and prayed. They felt so helpless. Sitting at the hospital and watching his daughter fight for her life was not how Mark imagined spending his first Father's Day. But as he sat there, he was filled with compassion as his daughter looked up at him and grasped his finger with her tiny hand.

"You always know how to get to your daddy's heart!" he said.

Mark recalled the many times Laura had given him "that look" with her eyes as if she wanted to hold hands. So Mark would extend his finger and she would grasp it. They held hands as long as Laura wanted to. Sometimes "holding hands" with his daughter meant being late for work, but Mark didn't mind. "Someday I'll teach you to ride a bike and fish. Hang in there, little girl!" he whispered.

Several transfusions and hours later the doctor announced, "The procedure worked! Go home and get a good night's rest!" But by the time the couple arrived home, the phone was ringing again. "Come back *now*!" the nurse exclaimed.

Mark and Karen arrived at the hospital just minutes after Laura had died. When they walked in, Laura's eyes were open and her hand was outstretched. *You were waiting for me,* Mark thought. He held his daughter and said good-bye. How he longed to tell her how much he missed her and how he wanted to help her more than anything in the world.

"Laura, I'll think of you waiting for me just like on Father's Day — with your eyes wide open and your hands outstretched. Until that day, please know that there will always be a place in my heart where you and I will be holding hands."

Mark knew that he could not, on this earth, hold the hands of his first two children. Would he even have a chance to hold the hand of little Sarah? "Dear God," he prayed, "how will I find the strength to endure this loss?"

The answer came. Holding hands with God was the only thing Mark could do. And so he did. Just as little Laura had reached out to him, Mark now reached out to God. He knew his grasp on God was tiny, but still he clung. He entrusted his remaining daughter's future into God's care.

Thirteen weeks later, Mark and Karen took Sarah home. They thanked God for their "miracle" as they sat on the sofa and held her. To their amazement, they discovered that Karen was pregnant again. A few days before Sarah's first birthday, God blessed them with Michael.

What an example of faith Mark and Karen are to me. Their journey through grief wasn't an easy one. Hiding, suffering, questioning, forgiving, and relating were all roadways of pain they walked through. But seeking God through pain and suffering was their consistent response. Maybe that's what helped them to move on and trust Him with the uncertainty of their future. Their actions have encouraged me to do the same — to reach out to God, place my uncertainty in His hands, and press on in my journey toward the future.

Are you willing to press on in your journey toward the future, or is it more comfortable to hide in a hole of despair? Does fear have a grip on you? Does the thought of losing another child hold you captive to the past? *It's too painful to try again! I'm afraid I'll lose another child*, you think.

I understand some of what you are feeling. After every loss I suffered deeply. That's why I allowed myself to journey through my grief at my own pace. So if you're not ready to face the future, that's okay. Seeking the future is just another part of the journey. It's up to you when you think you're ready to move on.

Is there hope after loss? Can faith overcome fear? Does God want you to trust Him and move on? Yes! But don't expect to feel as if "you're over your loss."

Be gentle with yourself. There will always be a part of your heart that holds hands with the child you never fully knew. You may still experience times when you cry, feel angry, or want to hide. That's okay. You lost a child, remember? But your loss has enlarged your life. Maybe you're more compassionate or less serious. Or perhaps you look at children as a gift now and don't take them for granted.

One thing is certain, you're not the same person you were. You've grown. Maybe it's time to grow some more. Are you ready to hold hands with the future? Look up.

God's eyes are open and they're looking at *you*. He's watched you fight and struggle through your pain. He was there all the time and wanted you to trust Him. He understands the anguish of your loss. He lost His Son too, remember? But His plan was that His loss would be our gain. He sent Jesus so that we could have eternal life.

Look up. His hand is outstretched. It's reaching for *you*. Please take it. Hold hands with Him and trust Him with your future. He *is* your future. There is nothing too big for Him. With Him all things are possible.

> *God, facing the future is hard for me. I'm afraid I might lose another child. I feel as if my past is holding me captive. My uncertainty and doubts enslave me. If I try again, will I fail? What if I can never have another child? Is a child really in my future plans? Only You know what my future*

holds. Help me to release my fear to You and replace it with faith. Even though I don't know what the future holds, I know who holds the future — You. Give me courage, Lord, as I take Your hand. Grasp it tightly, never let go. I want to spend eternity with You and walk toward it, starting today. You are my future. It feels good to hold hands with You. With You I know I can face anything. Amen.

Steps Toward Healing

1. Is your past holding you captive from the future? If so, how?
2. God wants to strengthen you and help you. In what ways can you allow Him to hold your hand? In what ways can you allow others to hold your hand?

M Y   P E R S O N A L   J O U R N E Y

JOURNEY THROUGH THE GALLERY OF PRAISE

• • •

Behold I will create
new heavens and a new earth.
The former things will not be remembered,
nor will they come to mind,
But be glad and rejoice forever
in what I will create.

ISAIAH 65:17—18A

PAINTINGS ADORN THE WALL of the museum. Each one is unique and tells a different story. Blue-green waves crash against the shore. Pastels and earth tones surround the cabin in the woods. Neon hues splash across the island sky. Golden flowers bloom on a cactus in the sand. Fluorescent zigzags of lightning illuminate the blackened sky behind a cross. White and yellow rays shine from the doorway of a tomb.

Can you hear the roar of the ocean? Can you feel the anger in the bolts behind the cross? Do you sense the peace and healing in the forest? Do you see hope beyond the empty tomb? You may feel as if your grief journey has led you to a gallery. Are the walls of your life adorned with emotional paintings of your grief that you've collected along the way?

Maybe you have one you've entitled "Anger." The canvas shows a raging hurricane. You painted it right after you lost your child. Is there another one you call "Forgiving"? It shows a meadow with a rainbow in the sky. Your paintings may look different from mine, brushed with colors, experiences, relationships, and places I've never encountered.

One of the paintings from my life's gallery was completed the day before Mother's Day in 1998. It shows three pine trees and a stump. Mother's Day can be a happy-sad day for me. Although I had one living child at that time, I also had four children in heaven.

So when the men arrived to trim our trees, it never occurred to me that God was in the process of completing a painting in my life. One of our thirty-foot pine trees had grown too close to the fence and was becoming bothersome to our neighbor. We decided to have it cut down. This was a poignant decision for me because I love trees. As the men climbed to the top branches of the pine tree, it suddenly dawned on me that this living tree would soon be destroyed.

The buzz of chain saws filled the air and branches thumped to the ground. Sorrow breezed through my soul. The death of this tree was triggering my personal sense of losses. I began to weep. "Stop!" I cried out to the men. "Don't cut down the entire tree!" The men looked surprised. "Please leave a stump!" I sniffled. I wanted something visible to show for my loss.

With tears streaming down my face I stared at my stump and prayed silently: *Lord, You are the Author of death and life. You are the Landscaper of my soul. I will give thanks and praise You in all circumstances!*

I knew this was a healing moment for me. I realized that the pathway to choose through pain that Mother's Day weekend was the path of praising. I felt as if I had new eyes and could see beyond the pain to the Person who was with me through the pain.

Then I noticed my stump was not alone. Three pine trees stood beside it. *How ironic!* I thought. *I've lost four children!* Amazingly, God gave me a loving reminder that He cared for me and understood the pain of my loss. He offered me a personal painting of three pine trees and a stump.

God calls you to examine each of the paintings of your grief and to find Him in each one. Is He your Comforter, Peace, Strength, Light, or Hope? Is He the Eye of the storm in the midst of your hurricane of anger or the God who keeps His rainbow of promises when you experience rainy days of grief. Go ahead! Look at your life's paintings. Now look beyond the paintings to who God is. Tell Him who He is to you. Repaint with new eyes, then journey through the gallery of praise.

God, my life is filled with emotional paintings I've collected along my grief journey. When I look at them, I recall my hurt and my pain. Give me new eyes. Help me see beyond each painting to who You are. I want to focus on You, not on my loss. You are the Creator of life and death. In my darkness, You are Light. In my fear, You are faithful. When I am confused, You are the Way. You are my Hope and Future. Help me seek You and journey through my gallery with praise. Amen.

Steps Toward Healing

1. The gallery of your life is filled with emotional paintings. Share about your painting for each of the stages of your journey — Hiding, Suffering, Questioning, and so on.
2. Now examine each painting. Do you see God there? Contemplate His strength in each of those areas. Praise Him for who He is. With your new eyes, perhaps a few new brush strokes are in order.

MY PERSONAL JOURNEY

Devotion 30

SEEKING OTHERS BEFORE YOU, BESIDE YOU, BEHIND YOU

• • •

You then, my son, be strong in the grace that is in Christ Jesus. And the things you have heard me say in the presence of many witnesses entrust to reliable men who will also be qualified to teach others. Endure hardship with us like a good soldier of Christ Jesus.

2 TIMOTHY 2:1–3

WHERE AM I GOING and how do I get there? wondered Traveler as she stared at the desolate road that seemed to slither endlessly through the dark, barren valley. Instinctively she knew she must travel this route, though she yearned for another. Accompanied by Loneliness and Uncertainty, Traveler hesitated, then stepped onto the road. Her mood reflected the thundering sky as she trudged forward.

Several miles into her journey, the sky was nearly black. "I'm so weary, I can't go on!" she moaned as she rounded the bend. To her amazement, she saw a moving figure in the distance. She squeezed Uncertainty's hand as she hastened her steps and squinted at the enlarging figure.

"Hello! Who are you? Can you help me in my journey?" she shouted.

To her surprise, the figure stopped. Traveler edged closer and sensed that something significant was about to happen. The figure turned and thrust a weathered, calloused hand into Traveler's. The person's grip was firm and confident, as if to communicate, "I've been on this road awhile and I know where I'm going!"

"I'm Mentor!"

"Nice to meet you, Mentor! I'm Traveler. Have you been on this journey long?"

Mentor nodded as she wiped the perspiration from her brow. "I'm familiar with this road," she said as she gazed deep into Traveler's eyes. "Looks like you could use some company. Do you want to walk with me for a while?"

Traveler sighed. A sense of calm flooded her soul as she paced her stride with Mentor's.

She felt free to laugh, to cry, to share, and to probe for answers to her questions. Mile after mile the duo trekked on. With each step Traveler felt more confident. Hearing about the battles won, the lessons learned, and the mistakes made in Mentor's journey was like healing balm on the wounds of her heart. When Traveler stumbled and fell, Mentor quickly helped her up again. "You can make it!" cheered Mentor. With renewed hope Traveler got back up and forged ahead, making sure to follow in Mentor's footsteps.

Night descended on the twosome and fear taunted Traveler. "Hold on, don't let go! I'll lead you!" Mentor exclaimed. Though weary, Traveler persevered and pressed on behind Mentor through the darkness to the sunrise.

The morning rays of sunshine revealed Others walking beside Traveler. *Where did they come from?* she wondered. Normally, Traveler would have ignored them, but something within her urged her to start a conversation. She was amazed to discover that she and Others had much in common. Traveler hastened her pace and was surprised at the confidence she felt. *Maybe I'm stronger because I'm not alone in my journey,* she thought. *I have someone in front of me to guide me and others beside me to relate to and encourage me.*

What more could I need? wondered Traveler.

As if on cue in response to her thought, a scream pierced the air. "Hello! I'm lost and I don't know where I'm going. Will you help me?"

Immediately Traveler stopped, turned, and looked at the path behind her. She knew what she must do.

Maybe you thought that your grief journey would be over when you finished this book. I wish that were true. It may get easier, and at times you may not even think about your loss and be the person leading and walking beside others. But don't be surprised when you experience an unexpected outburst and find yourself retracing your steps and crying out for help.

Your road of grief is personal. It is a continuous journey. The scenery may change through the years and you may become wiser, but be gentle with yourself and give yourself permission to give and receive support and guidance. God often teaches us more lessons when we think we've learned everything we possibly could about our loss. His desire is that you press on toward eternity with truth in your heart and hope in your step.

Maybe it's time to ask God to use your loss for good. He knows exactly where you are in your journey and will provide the right people to help you grow. Look around. God will show you who they are and will give you the courage and wisdom to reach out. Go ahead. You can do it!

God, thank You for providing others before me, beside me, and behind me in my grief journey to teach me and to help me grow. You understand how lonely the trek can be and how much I need to give and receive encouragement. Use my loss for good. In Your timing help me take the hand of someone who has lost a child and needs hope. Be my mentor and companion as You work through me. Help me seek You and follow You every step. Amen.

Steps Toward Healing

1. How can someone *before* you in grief guide you in your journey? Do you have someone *before you?* Share at least one way they've helped you.
2. Who are the people *beside* you? How do they support you?
3. Turn around, look back. Who has suffered loss and needs you to reach out to them? How will you help them?

MY PERSONAL JOURNEY

Devotion 31

I'LL KNOW MY CHILD IN HEAVEN

● ● ●

*And I heard a loud voice from the throne saying, "Now the dwelling of God is
with men, and he will live with them. They will be his people, and God himself
will be with them and be their God. He will wipe every tear from their eyes. There
will be no more death or mourning or crying or pain, for the old order of things
has passed away."*

REVELATION 21:3—4

*One thing I ask of the Lord,
   this is what I seek:
that I may dwell in the house of the LORD
   all the days of my life,
to gaze upon the beauty of the LORD. . . .
My heart says of you, "Seek his face!"
   Your face, Lord, I will seek.*

PSALM 27:4, 8

I'M LOOKING FORWARD TO heaven. No more corruption or death. No
more tears or grieving. Unconditional love, truth, and wholeness will be
the lifestyle. I'll be walking down streets of gold with a new body, heart,
and mind. Crystal water from the river of life will flow down the middle
of the street. And the Bible says there will even be trees!

Light will replace darkness. God himself will illuminate heaven. I will
experience perfect people in perfect fellowship. I can't even imagine
what that will feel like. What fun it will be to reunite with friends and
family who trusted Christ.

I wonder if Jesus will call me by name and welcome me personally
into paradise. With open arms and a loving smile, I can almost hear Him
say, "Welcome home, Kathe!"

I hope that four green-eyed, grinning boys holding balloons will be standing next to Him — the children I never knew, the children I grieved. "Hi, Mom!" they'll shout. We'll hug and kiss and then they'll take me by the hand and give me the heavenly tour. They'll introduce me to the angels, Moses, Hannah, the disciples, and Paul. I will fully comprehend that they preceded me to this eternal home. We'll stop and have a picnic under the tree of life.

Then they'll guide me through a grove of pine trees to a brand-new mansion. How good it will feel to walk up the steps and realize I'm home at last and I never have to leave. And when I look at the children I never knew on earth, I realize this time there will be no "good-byes," just an eternity praising God and getting to know them.

Heaven is a motivator to keep me pressing on in my journey through grief. Sometimes, like Paul in Philippians 1:23, my soul is homesick for my eternal home. Sometimes I long for those who have gone on ahead of me. Have you ever felt that way? What do you most look forward to in heaven? I bet you look forward to seeing Jesus too. Do you hope your child is standing next to Him, waiting to greet you?

Finally, you'll understand fully why God allowed your child to enter eternity before you. Your whole perspective on life and death and time will be made new. Your hiding, suffering, questioning, and need to forgive will vanish. The power of God's presence will overwhelm you. Your mourning will be replaced with dancing and eternal joy. You and I and the children we never knew will praise God for all of eternity.

Let's press on together in the journey to eternity!

God, thank You for creating heaven. I can hardly wait to reach the end of my journey and hear You say, "Welcome home!" Thank You for creating an eternal place with no death or tears for those who know You personally to live. I'm assured of spending eternity with You in heaven because I believe that I am a sinner and that Jesus died on the cross for my sins, was buried, and rose again. How awesome it will be to finally thank Jesus face-to-face for what He did for me. I hope my child will be waiting with Him to greet me. Thank You for allowing me all of eternity to get to know the child You always knew. Help me press on in my earthly journey and seek You first in everything I do. Use me to shine the hope of heaven to others. Amen.

Steps Toward Healing

1. What do you most look forward to about heaven?
2. What questions will you finally have answers to?
3. How has your perspective on the loss of your child been changed by God during your journey?

Read more about heaven: Isaiah 35:10; 65:17; Ezekiel 1:26–28; Luke 15:10; John 3:5–7; 14:2–3; 1 Corinthians 15:36–38; Philippians 3:20–21; 1 Thessalonians 4:16–17; 2 Timothy 4:8; Hebrews 12:22–23; Revelation 15:2–3; 20:1–22:5.

MY PERSONAL JOURNEY

_____

_____

_____

_____

_____

_____

_____

_____

_____

SHARING YOUR STORY

● ● ●

But in your hearts set apart Christ as Lord. Always be prepared to give an answer to everyone who asks you to give the reason for the hope that you have. But do this with gentleness and respect.

1 PETER 3:15

SHARING YOUR STORY CAN be a healing part of your journey. You may be thinking, *But it's too painful;* or, *Who would want to hear my story?* I'm amazed at the people I encounter at the grocery store, in our neighborhood, on an airplane, or through a friend of a friend who also lost a child and need personal encouragement. God knows exactly whom I need to meet. He may choose a small group setting for you to share your story, or He may choose for you to share with a large auditorium of people. What's important is having a willing heart to trust and obey Him when He calls you to share with someone.

Even though I frequently share with others, each time I share the story of my loss, my stomach churns and the scar of my heart rips open again. That's normal for me and keeps me relying on God's power. I have discovered that it is during those weak times that God does His best work. When I am weak, He is strong — and I become strong (see 2 Corinthians 12:7–10).

One day a woman stopped me in the parking lot and asked, "Oh, I see you had your baby?" I could tell she had no idea I had lost our child. (This happens frequently to me.) This was an opportunity to share my personal journey and share about God's sustaining power. Did anything spectacular occur? Not really, at least from my human viewpoint. But now, when I see her in the store, she knows my name and we always talk. To whom do you think she will turn if she or someone she knows encounters loss? And if she has questions about God…I hope she will seek me out too!

My husband and I have numerous stories of our "grief encounters" with others. God wants to work through me and use my story of losing a child to touch others and point them to Him. And He wants to do the same through you. What an awesome privilege we have. For me, it gives eternal purpose to my pain and validates the life of the child I never knew.

Get ready! When someone opens the door of conversation to talk about loss…share your story! The purpose in doing so is to give others hope in specific ways through your grief experience. When you share how God has worked in your life through your loss, you will encourage others.

How can you best prepare to share? My friend Carol Kent helped me to tell my story verbally and in written form through her Christian communication seminar and her book *Speak Up with Confidence: A Step-by-Step Guide for Speakers* (NavPress). Both tools give a practical "how-to" approach to communicate one's story. I've adapted her guidelines to help you begin writing your grief story in the blank pages that follow. In a sense "your story" will be the final devotion in this book. I've discovered that writing down my life lessons prepares me to speak them. Go ahead… you can do it!

Continue your journey! Share!

1. Start with prayer! Ask for God's wisdom and discernment in what to share.

2. Identify one personal experience in your journey through grief where God has worked through your life.

3. Briefly share what happened. Were you hiding, suffering, questioning, forgiving, relating, seeking?

4. What emotions did you experience? Did you feel angry, confused, sad, guilty, lonely, depressed, hopeless?

5. What spiritual lesson did you learn from it? If you were holding a grudge against your doctor, did God show the importance of forgiveness?

6. What Scripture verse or passage applies?

7. How can your story encourage others? Revisit your gallery of praise. Is there a painting hanging on the wall that could lead someone to praise God? Picture how God might use you. Here is one example of picturing the end result: "I want to help those who have lost a child understand the need to forgive others who have hurt them and the benefits of forgiving so that they will identify at least one person this week and practice forgiveness."

MY PERSONAL JOURNEY

MY PERSONAL JOURNEY

MY PERSONAL JOURNEY

MY PERSONAL JOURNEY

SUGGESTED RESOURCES

Books

Baker, Don. *Pain's Hidden Purpose*. Portland, Ore.: Multnomah, 1984.

Cacciatore, Joanne. *Passages*. Phoenix: MISS Publishing, 2000.

Cacciatore, Joanne. *Dear Cheyenne*. Phoenix: MISS Publishing, 1997.

Cloninger, Claire. *Postcards for People Who Hurt*. Dallas: Word, 1995.

De Pree, Max, *Dear Zoe*. San Francisco: HarperCollins, 1996.

DeYmaz, Linda. *Mommy, Please Don't Cry*. Gresham, Ore.: Vision, 1996.

Dobson, James. *When God Doesn't Make Sense*. Wheaton: Tyndale House, 1993.

Dravecky, Dave and Jan. *Do Not Lose Heart: Meditations of Encouragement and Comfort*. Grand Rapids: Zondervan, 1998.

Fitzgerald, Helen. *The Mourning Handbook: The Most Comprehensive Resource for Practical and Compassionate Advice on Coping with All Aspects of Death and Dying*. New York: Simon and Schuster, 1994.

Fitzpatrick, Carol. *A Time to Grieve*. Uhrichsville, Ohio.: Barbour, 1995.

Graham, Billy. *Facing Death — and the Life After*. Minneapolis: Grason, 1987.

Hayford, Jack. *I'll Hold You in Heaven*. Ventura, Calif.: Regal, 1986.

Huntley, Theresa. *Helping Children Grieve: When Someone You Love Dies*. Minneapolis: Augsburg, 1991.

Kent, Carol. *Mothers Have Angel Wings*. Colorado Springs: NavPress, 1995.

Kent, Carol. *Secret Longings of the Heart*. Colorado Springs: NavPress, 1992.

Kinnaman, Gary. *My Companion Through Grief*. Ann Arbor: Servant, 1996.

Lewis, C. S. *A Grief Observed*. San Francisco: Harper & Row, reprinted 1989.

Miles, Margaret Shandor. *The Grief of a Parent When a Child Dies*. Oak Brook, Ill.: Compassionate Friends, 1978.

Myers, Ruth. *31 Days of Praise*. Sisters, Ore.: Multnomah, 1994.

NIV Encouragement Bible: The Answer for Those Who Hurt. With features compiled by Dave and Jan Dravecky and Joni Eareckson Tada. Grand Rapids: Zondervan, 2001.

Pink, Michael and Brenda. *Grace for Grief*. Grand Rapids: World, 1995.

Rank, Maureen. *Free to Grieve*. Minneapolis: Bethany, 1985.

Sittser, Gerald. *A Grace Disguised: How the Soul Grows Through Loss*. Grand Rapids: Zondervan, 1996.

Smith, Hannah Whitall. *The God of All Comfort*. Chicago: Moody, 1956.

Strannigan, Shawn Alyne. *Someday We'll Play in Heaven*. Cincinnati: Standard, 1995.

Vredevelot, Pam. *Empty Arms*. Sisters, Ore.: Multnomah, 1984.

Waltman, Dawn Siegrist, *A Rose in Heaven*. Paradise, Pa.: Paradise Publications, 1999.

Westberg, Granger. *Good Grief*. Philadelphia: Fortress, 1972.

Wunnenberg, Kathe. *Grieving the Loss of a Loved One*. Grand Rapids: Zondervan, 2000.

Yancey, Philip. *Where Is God When It Hurts?* Grand Rapids: Zondervan, 1977.

Magazines

Bereavement Magazine. Colorado Springs, Colorado. (719) 266-0006.

Music

Aaron, Jeoffrey. "After the Rain," "Beyond." From *After the Rain*, Star Song, 1996.

Becker, Margaret. "I Will Be with You." From *Soul*, Sparrow, 1993.

Beyond the Blue. "Reason for the Rain." From *Beyond the Blue*, Word, 1996.

Brunsting, Karen. *From Tragedy to Triumph — The Concert*. Self-published. (231) 652-6349.

Chapman, Steven Curtis. "With Hope." From *Speechless*, Sparrow, 1999.

Greens, The. "Jesus' Rocking Chair." From *Jesus' Rocking Chair*, Benson, 1994.

Keaggy, Cheri. "My Faith Will Stay," "Keep on Shinin'," "Lay It Down." From *My Faith Will Stay*, Sparrow, 1996.

Kenoly, Ron. "Mourning into Dancing." From *Lift Him Up*, Hosanna Music, 1992.

Krippayne, Scott. "Every Single Tear." From *Bright Star Blue Sky*, Spring Hill Records, 1999.

Lewis, Crystal. "Beauty for Ashes." From *Beauty for Ashes*, Myrrh Records, 1996.

Meece, David. "Brokenness, Inside Out." From *Once in a Lifetime*, Star Song, 1993.

Moore, Kim. "God Makes No Mistakes." From *Beyond Redemption*, Heart's Desire Music, 1996.

Paris, Twila. "Hold On," "I Am Not Afraid Anymore," "I Will Listen." From *Where I Stand*, Sparrow, 1996.

Paris, Twila. "A Visitor from Heaven." From *Beyond a Dream*, Sparrow, 1993.

Point of Grace. "Jesus Will Still Be There." From *Point of Grace*, Word, 1993.

Thum, Pam. "Feel the Healing." From *Feel the Healing*, Benson, 1995.

Troccoli, Kathy. "Good-bye for Now." From *Corner of Eden*, Reunion Records, 1998.

Various Artists. "Hold Me, Jesus." From *Awesome God—A Tribute to Rich Mullins*, Reunion Records, 1998.

SUPPORT ORGANIZATIONS

Abiding Hearts
Maria La Fond-Budge
P.O. Box 904
Libby, Montana 59923
Phone: (406) 293-4416
Web site: www.abidinghearts.com; www.imt.net~hearts
Providing support to caregivers, family, and parents who desire to continue pregnancy after adverse prenatal diagnosis

AMEND
(Aiding Mothers [and Fathers] Experiencing Neonatal Death)
Maureen Connelly
4324 Berrywick Terrace
St. Louis, MO 63128
Phone: (314) 487-7582
Providing volunteer one-on-one peer counseling for those who have experienced miscarriage, stillbirth, or neonatal death

Anencephaly Support Foundation
20311 Sienna Pines Court
Spring, TX 77379
Phone: (888) 206-7526
E-mail: asf@asfhelp.com
Web site: www.asfhelp.com

Bereavement Services
Gunderson Lutheran (Medical Foundation)
1910 South Avenue
La Crosse, WI 54601
Phone: (800) 362-9567   ext. 4747
E-mail: berservs@gundluth.org
Web site: www.gundluth.org/bereave
Providing training and support materials to healthcare professionals working with parents who have lost a baby during pregnancy or shortly after birth

Christian Family Care Agency
3603 N. 7th Ave.
Phoenix, AZ 85013-3638
Phone: (602) 234-1935
Web site: www.cfcare.org
Mission is to demonstrate God's love by providing child and family counseling, foster care, pregnancy support counseling and support, and adoption services

Christian Medical and Dental Association
501 5th St.
Bristol, TN 37620
Web site: www.cmdahome.org
Providing "Prescribe-A-Resource" catalog and doctor referrals

CLIMB (Center for Loss In Multiple Birth, Inc.)
P.O. Box 91377
Anchorage, AK 99509
Phone: (907) 222-5321
E-mail: climb@pobox.alaska.net
Web site: www.climb-support.org

The Compassionate Friends
P.O. Box 3696
Oak Brook, IL 60522-3696
Phone: (630) 990-0010
Web site: www.compassionatefriends.org

Dravecky's Outreach of Hope
13840 Geneagle Drive
Colorado Springs, CO 80921

The Emily Center
Phoenix Children's Hospital
909 E. Brill St.
Phoenix, AZ 85006
Phone: (602) 239-6902
E-mail: emilyc@phxchildrens.com
Web site: www.phxchildrens.com (programs: Emily Center)
A partner in your search for child health information

Hannah's Prayer
Internet based Christian Infertility and Pregnancy/Infant Loss Support
P.O. Box 5016
Auburn, CA 95604–5016
E-mail: hannahs@hannah.org
Web site: www.hannah.org

M.I.S.S. (Mothers in Sympathy & Support)
P.O. Box 5333
Peoria, AZ 85385
Web site: www.misschildren.org

National SIDS Resource Center
Phone: (703) 821-8955

NORD (National Organization for Rare Disorders)
P.O. Box 8923
New Fairfield, CT 06812
Phone: (800) 999-NORD
E-mail: orphan@nord.rdb.com

Perinatal Loss
2116 NE 18ᵗʰ Ave.
Portland, OR 97212
Phone: (503) 284-7426
Web site: www.tearsoup.com

A Place to Remember
1885 University Ave.
St. Paul, MN 55104
Phone: (800) 631-0973
Web site: www.aplacetoremember.com

Pregnancy & Infant Loss Center
1421 E. Wayzata Blvd.
Wayzata, MN 55391
Phone: (612) 473-9372
Web site: www.pilc.org

Resolve

1310 Broadway
Somerville, MA 02114-1779
Phone: (617) 623-0744
E-mail: info@resolve.org
Web site: www.resolve.org
Education, support, and resources for those experiencing infertility

SHARE, Pregnancy & Infant Loss, Inc.

St. Joseph's Health Center
300 First Capitol Dr.
St. Charles, MO 63301
Phone: (800) 821-6819
E-mail: share@nationalshareoffice.com
Web site: www.nationalshareoffice.com

SIDS (Sudden Infant Death Syndrome Alliance)

Phone: (800) 221-7437

Stepping Stones
C/o Bethany Christian Services

P.O. Box 294
Grand Rapids, MI 49501-0294
Phone: (616) 224-7488

E-mail: step@bethany.org

Web site: www.bethany.org/step

A newsletter with Christ-centered articles for those experiencing infertility.

Dear Friend:

Thank you for taking the time to journey with me through my book. As you continue your journey through grieving the child you never knew, I pray you will have renewed perspective and hope. Your child matters. Take a moment right now and add your child's name to the dedication section at the front of the book.

I would love to hear from you. E-mail me at hopeforyou@cox.net, or write to me at P.O. Box 50995, Phoenix, AZ 85076-0995.

If you are interested in my speaking for your group, please call Gene or Carol Kent at Speak Up Speaker Services: (810) 982-0898, or e-mail them at speakupinc@aol.com.

May God continue to meet you where you are and make His presence known to you.

> Hugs from my heart to yours.
> Kathe Wunnenberg (Proverbs 3:5–6)

GRIEVING THE LOSS
OF A LOVED ONE
KATHE WUNNENBERG

Another book by Kathe Wunnenberg, to encourage anyone who has lost someone they love …

The bottom has dropped out of your life. Will the ache ever cease, the tears ever stop?

How can you go on in the face of a grief so profound?

Kathe Wunnenberg knows the terrible pain of losing your loved one and she understands that the sense of loss never really goes away. Yet as surely as God is faithful, there is hope for your broken heart to mend. There is life beyond the sorrow. As hard as it might be to believe right now, there is even the promise of joy in due season as you walk through your grief one day at a time.

Grieving the Loss of a Loved One is a collection of devotions especially for you, especially for now. You will find this book to be a wise, understanding, and comforting companion to help you grieve in the ways you must, and to encourage you that God has not forsaken you.

- Includes a Scripture passage and prayer for each devotion
- Offers readings for holidays, birthdays, and special occasions
- Provides space for journalizing after each devotion

Hardcover 0-31022778-X

Pick up a copy today at your favorite bookstore!

We want to hear from you. Please send your comments about this book to us in care of the address below. Thank you.

GRAND RAPIDS, MICHIGAN 49530 USA

WWW.ZONDERVAN.COM